Every
Second
Counts

Also by Lance Armstrong
with Sally Jenkins

It's Not About the Bike:
My Journey Back to Life

Every
Second
Counts

Lance Armstrong

with Sally Jenkins

Broadway Books
New York

To Luke, Grace, and Isabelle
for always reminding me that every second really does count

Acknowledgments

The authors would like to offer their deeply felt thanks to the following people, without whom this book could not have been started, and certainly would never have been completed.

Bill Stapleton, Bart Knaggs, and Lee Walker offered unvarnished advice and their ever-sure friendship. Jim Ochowicz, Dr. Craig Nichols, Johan Bruyneel, George Hincapie, Jeff Garvey, and Doug Ullman gave the same, as well as their conscientious service to various causes. Sally Reed and everyone at the foundation are a constant example. Countless other friends, including Scott MacEachern, Dave Mingey, and Ryan Street, offered their memories and perspectives. Stacy Creamer of Broadway Books was her usual generous and tremendously patient editor-self, and Stuart Calderwood's care of the manuscript was invaluable.

But they will all understand when I say that my greatest thanks go to my family and to my team, Big Blue.

CHAPTER 1

Pitched Back

So, it looks as though I'm going to live—at least for another 50 years or more. But whenever I need to reassure myself of this, as I sometimes do, I go out to a place called Dead Man's Hole, and I stare down into it, and then, with firm intent, I strip off my shirt and I leap straight out into what you might call the great sublime.

Let's say it's my own personal way of checking for vital signs. Dead Man's Hole is a large green mineral pool gouged out of a circular limestone cliff, so deep into the hill country of Texas that it's hardly got an address. According to conflicting legends, it's either where Confederates tossed Union sympathizers to drown, or where Apaches lured unsuspecting cowboys who didn't see the fall coming. In any event, I'm drawn to it, so much so that I bought 200 acres of brush and pasture surrounding it, and I've worn a road into the dirt by driving out there. It seems only right that a place called Dead Man's Hole should belong to a guy who nearly died—and who, by the way, has no intention of just barely living.

I stand there next to a 45-foot waterfall and examine the drop—

and myself, while I'm at it. It's a long drop, so long that it makes the roof of my mouth go dry just looking at it. It's long enough for a guy to actually think on the way down, and to think more than one thought, too. Long enough to think first one thing, *A little fear is good for you*, and then another, *It's good for you if you can swim*, and then one more thing as I hit the water: *Oh fuck, it's cold*. As I jump, there are certain unmistakable signs that I'm alive: the press of my pulse, the insistent sound of my own breathing, and the whanging in my chest that's my heart, which by then sounds like an insubordinate prisoner beating on the bars of my ribcage.

I come up whooping through the foam and swim for the rocks. Then I climb back up and towel off, and I drive home to my three kids. I burst through the door, and I shout at my son, Luke, and my twin daughters, Grace and Isabelle, and I kiss them on the necks, and I grab a Shiner Bock beer with one hand and an armful of babies with the other.

The first time I ever did it, my wife, Kik, just looked at me and rolled her eyes. She knew where I'd been.

"Was that clarifying for you?" she said.

At what point do you let go of not dying? Maybe I haven't entirely and maybe I don't want to.

I know they're out there, lying in their hospital beds, with those damn drip poles, watching the damn chemo slide into their veins, and thinking, *This guy had the same thing I do. If he can do it, I can, too*. I think of them all the time.

My friend Lee Walker says I got "pitched back." What he

means is, I almost died, and possibly even did die a little, but then I got pitched back into the world of the living. It's as good a description as any of what happened. I was 25 when cancer nearly killed me: advanced choriocarcinoma spread to my abdomen, lungs, and brain and required two surgeries and four cycles of chemotherapy to get rid of. I wrote an entire book about death, called *It's Not About the Bike*, about confronting the possibility of it, and narrowly escaping it.

"Are you sure?" I asked the doctor.

"I'm sure."

"How sure?"

"I'm very sure."

"How can you be so sure?"

"I'm so sure that I've scheduled you for surgery at 7 A.M. tomorrow."

Mounted on a light table, the X-ray showed my chest. Black meant clear; white meant cancer. My chest looked like a snowstorm.

What I didn't and couldn't address at the time was the prospect of life. Once you figure out you're going to live, you have to decide how to, and that's not an uncomplicated matter. You ask yourself: *now that I know I'm not going to die, what will I do? What's the highest and best use of my self?* These things aren't linear, they're a mysterious calculus. For me, the best use of myself has been to race in the Tour de France, the most grueling sporting event in the world.

Every time I win another Tour, I prove that I'm alive—and therefore that others can survive, too. I've survived cancer again, and again, and again, and again. I've won four Tour titles, and I wouldn't mind a record-tying five. That would be some good living.

But the fact is that I wouldn't have won even a single Tour de

France without the lesson of illness. What it teaches is this: pain is temporary. Quitting lasts forever.

To me, just finishing the Tour de France is a demonstration of survival. The arduousness of the race, the sheer unreasonableness of the job, the circumnavigation of an entire country on a bicycle, village to village, along its shores, across its bridges, up and over the mountain peaks they call cols, requires a matchless stamina. The Tour is so taxing that Dutch rider Hennie Kuiper once said, after a long climb up an alp, "The snow had turned black in my eyes." It's not unlike the stamina of people who are ill every day. The Tour is a daily festival of human suffering, of minor tragedies and comedies, all conducted in the elements, sometimes terrible weather and sometimes fine, over flats, and into headwinds, with plenty of crashes. And it's three weeks long. Think about what you were doing three weeks ago. It feels like last year.

The race is very much like living—except that its consequences are less dire and there's a prize at the end. Life is not so neat.

There was no pat storybook ending for me. I survived cancer and made a successful comeback as a cyclist by winning the 1999 Tour, but that was more of a beginning than an end. Life actually went on, sometimes in the most messy, inconvenient, and untriumphant ways. In the next five years I'd have three children, take hundreds of drug tests (literally), break my neck (literally), win some more races, lose some, too, and experience a breakdown in my marriage. Among other adventures.

When you walk into the Armstrong household, what you see is infants crawling everywhere. Luke was born in the fall of 1999 to Kristin (Kik) Armstrong and me shortly after that first Tour, and the twins came in the fall of 2001. Grace and Isabelle have blue saucer eyes, and they toddle across the floor at scarcely believable speeds. They like to pull themselves upright on the available furniture and stand there, wobbling, while they plan how to make trouble. One of Isabelle's amusements is to stand up on the water dispenser and press the tap until the kitchen floods, while she laughs hysterically. I tell her, "No, no, no," and she just shakes her head back and forth and keeps laughing, while the water runs all over the floor. I can't wait for their teen years.

Luke adds to the bedlam by riding his bike in the living room, or doing laps in a plastic car, or tugging the girls around in separate red wagons. He is sturdy and hardheaded. He wears his bike helmet inside the house and refuses to take it off, even when we go out to dinner. We get some interesting stares—but anything is better than the fight that ensues if you try to remove the helmet. He insists on wearing it just in case he might get to go cycling with me. To him, a road is what his father does for a living. I'm on the road so much that when the phone rings, he says, "Daddy."

One afternoon I went to pick my family up at an airport. Luke gave me a long stare and said, "Daddy, you look like me."

"Uh, I look like *you*?" I said.

"Yeah."

"Are you sure it's not the other way around?"

"Yeah, I'm sure. It's definitely you that looks like me."

Also milling around our house are a cat named Chemo and a small white dog named Boone. I trip around all of them, watching my feet, careful not to step on a critter or a kid. It's been a chaotic few years, and not without its casualties. There have been so many children and adults and animals to feed that sometimes things get confused and the dog winds up with the baby food. One day Kik handed me what was supposed to be a glass of water.

"This tastes like Sprite," I said.

"Just drink it," she said.

I could never seem to find the right keys to anything. One time I pulled the ring of keys from my pocket and stared at them in their seeming hundreds, and said to Kik, wonderingly, "I have the keys to the whole world." She just said, "Perfect."

The reason I have so many keys is because I need so many homes and vehicles, in various countries and counties. I spend most of the spring and summer in my European home in Girona, Spain, while I prepare for the Tour. When the racing season is over, I come back to Austin. Our family lives in a house in central Austin, and we also have the ranch in the hill country. But my favorite home is a small hideaway, a one-room cabin just outside Austin, in the hills overlooking the Colorado River. Across the river there's a rope swing dangling from an old bent oak, and on hot days I like to swing on the rope and hurl myself into the current.

I love the tumult of my large family, and I've even been accused of fostering a certain amount of commotion, because I have no tolerance for peace and quiet. I'm congenitally unable to sit still; I crave action, and if I can't find any, I invent it.

My friends call me Mellow Johnny. It's a play on the French term for the leader of the Tour de France, who wears a yellow jersey: the *maillot jaune.* We like to joke that Mellow Johnny is the Texan pronunciation. The name is also a play on my not-so-mellow personality. I'm Mellow Johnny, or Johnny Mellow, or, if you're feeling formal, Jonathan Mellow.

Sometimes I'm just Bike Boy. I ride my bike almost every day, even in the off-season, no matter the weather. It could be hailing, and my friends and riding partners dread the call that they know is going to come: they pick up the phone, and they hear Bike Boy on the other end, demanding, "You ridin', or you *hidin*'?"

One famous November day during the off-season, I rode four and a half hours through one of the strongest rainstorms on record. Seven inches of precipitation, with flash floods and road closures everywhere. I loved it. People thought I was crazy, of course. But when I'm on the bike, I feel like I'm 13 years old. I run fewer red lights now, but otherwise it's the same.

Some days, though, I feel much older than a man in his thirties; it's as if I've lived a lot longer. That's the cancer, I guess. I've spent a lot of time examining what it did to me—how it aged me, altered me—and the conclusion I've come to is, it didn't just change my body; it changed my mind.

I've often said cancer was the best thing that ever happened to me. But everybody wants to know what I mean by that: how could a life-threatening disease be a good thing? I say it because my illness was also my antidote: it cured me of laziness.

Before I was diagnosed, I was a slacker. I was getting paid a lot of money for a job I didn't do 100 percent, and that was more than just a shame—it was wrong. When I got sick, I told myself: if I get another chance, I'll do this right—and I'll work for something more than just myself.

I have a friend, a fellow cancer survivor named Sally Reed, who sums up the experience better than anyone I know. "My house is burned down," she says, "but I can see the sky."

Sally was diagnosed with rampant breast cancer in the spring of 1999. The disease had reached Stage Three and spread to her lymphatic system. She was facing both radiation and chemotherapy. Right away, all of her smaller fears disappeared, replaced by this new one. She had been so afraid of flying that she hadn't flown in more than 15 years. But after she got the diagnosis, she called an airline and booked a flight to Niagara Falls. She went there by herself and stood overlooking the roaring falls.

"I wanted to see something bigger than me," she says.

Mortal illness, like most personal catastrophes, comes on suddenly. There's no great sense of foreboding, no premonition, you just wake up one morning and something's wrong in your lungs, or your liver, or your bones. But near-death cleared the decks, and what came after was a bright, sparkling awareness: time is limited, so I better wake up every morning fresh and know that I have just one chance to live this particular day right, and to string my days together into a life of action, and purpose.

If you want to know what keeps me on my bike, riding up an alp for six hours in the rain, that's your answer.

Oddly enough, while the near-death experience was clarifying, the success that came afterward was confusing.

It complicated life significantly, and permanently. The impact of winning the 1999 Tour de France was larger than I ever imagined it would be, from the first stunned moment when I stepped off the plane in Austin, into the Texas night air, to see people there waiting. There was yellow writing painted on the streets, "*Vive la Lance*," and banners stretched across the streets, and friends had decorated our entire house with yellow flowers, streamers, and balloons. I was bewildered to be invited to the State Capitol to see our then-governor, George W. Bush, and afterward there was a parade through town with more than 6,000 cyclists (in yellow) leading the route. People were lined up five deep along the sides, waving signs and flags.

I didn't understand it: I was just another Austin bike geek who liked his margaritas and his Tex-Mex, and Americans weren't supposed to care about cycling. "You don't get it," said my friend and agent, Bill Stapleton.

I lived in a constant, elevated state of excitement; the air was thin and getting thinner, and compounding the excitement was the fact that Kik and I were awaiting the birth of our first child, Luke. I kept waiting for things to subside, but they never did—they just got busier. Bill was swamped with offers and requests and proposed endorsements. He struck some handsome new deals on my behalf, with prestigious sponsors like Bristol-Myers Squibb, Nike, and Coca-Cola. With the deals came new responsibilities: I shot half a dozen commercials, posed for magazine ads and the Wheaties box. I earned the nickname "Lance Incorporated" and now I was a business entity instead of just a person.

It was estimated that the '99 victory generated $50 million in global media exposure for the United States Postal Service cycling team. Our budget grew, and now we were a $6 million year-round enterprise with dozens of support staff, mechanics, cooks, and accountants.

With success came the problem of celebrity, and how not to be distorted by it. There were invitations that left me and Kik amazed. Robin Williams had a jet. Kevin Costner offered his house in Santa Barbara. Elton John had a Super Bowl party. Kik and I felt like Forrest Gump, lurking in the background of photos with accomplished people. We were impressed, so much so that sometimes we would save the messages on our answering machine and replay them, awed.

But fame, I learned, is an isotope, and it's not good for you. When you become celebrated, a kind of unhealthy radioactive decay forms around you, and the decay can be creeping, or even catastrophic. The attention could become addictive. There was no doubt I could have turned into a swollen-headed jerk, and there's no doubt some people think I did turn into one, much as I tried to keep it all straight.

One afternoon I said, "Bono called me."

Kik said, "Really? Brad Pitt called me. He wants to know what time we're having lunch."

Okay, I got it.

I struggled with what to think about all of it, until I read a remark by J. Craig Ventner, the man who helped map the human genome. He said, "Fame is an intrinsic negative. People respond to you based on their preconceived notion of you, and that puts you at a continual disadvantage." I agreed. I was just the son of a single mother from Plano, Texas, a secretary who'd passed on her conscientious work ethic. It seemed wrong to be idolized by strangers, or to idolize strangers in turn: I preferred to idolize my mother, or my teammates. They were the people I'd pick to go through hard times with.

Don't get me wrong—I liked what winning the Tour did for me, as a person, and as an athlete, and for my family. It made life very comfortable, and I was thankful for that. But I was learning that not all of the people who flew to Paris to be at the finish line were my very best friends. And I was learning that the only thing wealth meant was that you had a lot of money. If you thought of fame and wealth any other way, you could get confused—think you achieved it through some specialness and believe it made you better than others, or smarter.

There was one good use for celebrity: it was a huge and influential platform from which to lobby for the cancer cause. I had become a symbol, the poster boy for the hardships of the disease, and now I was on cereal boxes, and *Late Night with David Letterman*, and I went to the White House.

At first I didn't quite understand the intensity of people's curiosity. What did they care about my particular hurts? But one day Kik said, "You've been on the brink, stood on the edge between life and death and looked over. You've seen the view from that cliff and come back down. You can share that perspective."

The pitched-back experience, I realized, was important: even to participate in the Tour demonstrated that I had survived, and if I had survived, *others could, too*. What's more, they could live the rest of their lives normally, if not even better than before.

It was an important message for the entire cancer community, not just for patients but for families, physicians, and nurses dealing with the disease. Doctors knew how serious my situation had been, and how severe my four cycles of chemotherapy had been, and they knew that (a) I survived it and (b) the treatment didn't ruin my body. That gave the doctors hope, and it occurred to me that doctors needed hope as much as patients did.

They wanted to use me as an example, and I wanted to be used. But I wanted to be used in the right way. I was deeply uncomfortable with the word "hero"—it wasn't heroic to survive cancer. No one was immune; eight million Americans suffered from some form of it, and about a million were newly diagnosed each year. Like them, I was dealt an unfortunate hand, and I simply did what came naturally to me: I tried hard.

I met all kinds of people who were fighting the illness, turned yellow and gaunt by chemotherapy. Go to Sloan-Kettering in New York, or M. D. Anderson in Houston, or the Southwest Regional Cancer Clinic in Austin, and you'll see them, 50 or 60 people packed into a waiting room that only has 30 chairs, people of the widest possible variety, and a handful of stone-faced, weary nurses.

Other cancer patients wanted to know everything I did, every drug I took, every morsel I digested.

"What was in your chemo?"

"What did you eat?"

"What kind of vitamins did you take?"

"How much did you ride your bike?"

I was a success story—for the moment. But if I got sick again, I would no longer be a success story, and the truth was, at times I was still as scared and anxious as a patient. What if the cancer came back? Each time I visited a hospital I had an uneasy reaction. The first thing that struck me was the smell. If I did a smell test I could find a hospital with my eyes closed: disinfectant, medicine, bad cafeteria food, and recycled air through old vents, stale and artificial. And the lighting: a leaky radiant, it made everyone look pale, like they didn't have quite enough blood in their bodies. The sounds were artificial and grating: the squeak of the nurses' rubber-soled shoes, the sound of the hospital mattresses. A hospital mattress is covered with plastic, and I remembered how it felt and sounded as I shifted in the bed, the crackle of the covering beneath me, every time I moved, crackle, crackle, wrinkle, wrinkle.

These are the odors and sensations and images that all cancer patients carry with them no matter how far removed they are from the disease, and they are so traumatic, so concentrated, that they can bring about reactions years afterward.

Some people even get physically ill when they encounter sights or smells that remind them of illness. There was a story in the *New England Journal of Medicine*: a woman was treated for breast cancer with very arduous chemo, and she suffered violent bouts of nausea. Five years later, she was walking in a mall when she ran into her oncologist, the doctor who had treated her. She threw up. So that's how cancer stays with you. And it has stayed with me.

When I had the illness, I fought it with the hope of returning to my life, but I never gave any real thought to what that life would be. The term "life after cancer" has very real ramifications: you might be dealing with the loss of a leg or a breast, or with infertility, or, as in my own case, with sterility, a potentially lost career, and deep anxieties. There are physical, emotional, and financial consequences. In other words, you can save someone's life, but what about saving the *quality* of that life?

All of these issues fell under the title "survivorship," a curious, post-traumatic state of being that I was experiencing, and which all cancer survivors experience in one form or another. Survivorship, I decided, should be the core of the cancer foundation I'd launched: managing the illness and its aftereffects was as important as fighting it. The Lance Armstrong Foundation began to take shape as a place where people could come for information of the most personal and practical kind. There were other, richer foundations and more comprehensive Web sites, but at the LAF, hopefully you could call or e-mail us and get a greeting card from me to a patient, or you could ask, what's the right exercise for breast-cancer patients and survivors?

Most people, I discovered, just wanted to be heard, or sometimes they just wanted to be touched. I met a boy named Cameron Stewart who has leukemia, got it when he was about six.

"Did you have a port?" he asked me.

"Did I have a port? Look at this," I said.

I unbuttoned my shirt and showed him the scar on my chest. He took off his shirt, too. He had a small port inserted in his tiny little bird chest.

Cameron and I have kept in touch; he came to Austin with his family for our annual foundation bike race. He's in remission, and he's growing into a healthy kid. He likes to say, "I have Lance Armstrong legs."

I met other athletes with cancer, and we swapped stories and anecdotes. I laughed with Eric Davis, the great baseball player, about trying to eat during chemo. "Caesar salad with chicken," he said. "I ate two of them, every day, right before the chemo. Because when you take chemo, you throw up. And if you don't have anything in you, you can't throw up. And *not* being able to throw up is even worse than throwing up. So I'd eat my Caesar salad. It went in, just so it could come out."

Doctors got cancer, too. A prominent physician in New York was diagnosed with prostate cancer. We got to know each other via e-mail. He wrote, "I hope I live for ten more years." I wrote him back: "I hope you were joking about living only ten years," I said. "I'll see you in thirty."

I never tired of the subject, of talking about it or hearing about it or reliving it. I celebrated the three-year anniversary of my diagnosis on October 2, 1999, and I called it "Carpe Diem Day," meaning, "Seize the Day." It remained the most important day of the year, larger than any birthday or anniversary or holiday, and it was a day filled with introspection, of thinking about second chances.

Every so often a friend or a family member discovered just how much cancer occupied my mind. One afternoon my coach, Chris Carmichael, told me that he had begun working with other athletes who had cancer. Chris wanted my counsel. "You have a great template for me to work from," he said. "You've been there, you know exactly what those athletes are facing." I did: the long days with an IV in the arm, the heaving nausea, and the scars and chemical burns that would tattoo their bodies. But I didn't feel like an expert on how to beat cancer, I just felt lucky.

"You don't know, this thing could come back tomorrow, come back in me," I said to Chris. "It only went away because mine was treatable. But it's not really gone and it's not something that ever does disappear. I still worry about it."

"Lance, it's not coming back," he said.

"Who says? Who says it can't come back?"

At no point could I say, "That's over." Even with a Tour victory, and a new baby on the way, I still had the lingering impression that everything might go away overnight, that I might not be able to ride again, or even that I'd get sick again.

My son came in the early hours of a mid-October morning, and his birth was hectic and difficult: at first, he had trouble breathing and the nurses took him away to clear his lungs. Finally, he let go a beautiful howl.

The fear at that moment when he wasn't breathing trumped any fear I'd ever known. Kik and I looked at each other, and we instantly realized the truth about parenthood: it's the most vulnerable state in the world. Later, Kik said, "Now we're both capable of being emotionally annihilated." To be a parent was to be totally stripped down, emotionally naked, and that would be true for the rest of our lives.

After Luke was cleaned and wrapped in a blanket, we settled into a room to get some rest. But the reverberations and anxieties lasted all night and made it impossible to sleep. I shifted on the plastic hospital mattress. I thought about the difference in the fear I had for myself during cancer, and the fear I had for someone else's well-being now that I was a father.

I thought about my mother, and wondered at the risks she had watched me take without interfering, the things she had watched me climb, the high dives and hard falls, the times I wrecked my bike, and of course, the time I got sick. Nothing could be as emotionally hazardous, or interesting, or rewarding, as the job of being a parent.

Having a child was an excellent way to feel alive, I decided. Not unlike jumping off a cliff.

Cancer made me want to do more than just live: it made me want to live in a certain way. The near-death experience stripped something away. Where others have a little bit of trepidation—*Am I ready for a child, what happens if people don't like me, should I do this or is it too dangerous*—I didn't anymore. To me, there were some lives where you might as well be dead. Illness had left me with a clear view of the difference between real fear and mere disquiet, and of everything worth having, and doing.

The trick was to make sure it wasn't also a recipe for disaster. I was a confirmed risk-taker, but now I was also a husband, father, and businessman responsible for others. Did that mean I had to make concessions, become more conservative? It was an essential question. I wanted to live a life of action, but I also wanted to live a life of vigilance.

It was an uneasy balance, much easier in theory than in practice. I wanted to be a father—and I also wanted a motorcycle. My friends lectured me to slow down; for years my pal John Korioth had been yelling at me to drive more slowly. Korioth was the best man at our wedding, and we call him "College," which is short for College Boy. We call him that because he played college basketball, and one night he and another of my best friends, Bart Knaggs, got into a beer-fueled game of one-on-one. Bart started taunting John. "Come on, College," he said, "let's see you make one." He's been College to us ever since.

When I had a Porsche, before the birth of my kids, College was always begging me to ease off the accelerator. I'd roar down the freeways, while he flinched in the passenger seat, white-knuckled and cussing in anger. "Son of a bitch!" he'd scream, "Slow down!" I'd just die laughing.

I also thought it was hysterically funny to make him turn pale on bike rides. We would ride out to a place called Red Bud Trail, where there's a hill that sweeps down into a blind left-hand turn. I'd descend the hill at high speed, swing wide into the opposite lane, and

1 8   Lance Armstrong

then suddenly dive into the turn. It scared him every time. I explained to him that compared to a high-speed mountain descent, it was an elementary move, and it looked much more dangerous than it really was. But College didn't believe me, until one day in France I showed him what race-pace was really like. One minute we were gliding down an alp, side by side. The next minute I was gone, rocketing downhill into the mist. He's never bothered me again about Red Bud Trail.

But with the arrival of children, I've reprioritized. I got rid of the Porsche in favor of a family-friendly car. Not long ago, a gentleman invited me to tour a Ferrari factory.

"You don't understand," I said, "I need something with three baby seats."

College claims that the craziest and most dangerous thing I do these days is argue with truckers, and he might be right. Over the years, I've been run off the road by too many pickups and rock trucks to count. Texas truck drivers hate cyclists; we have an ongoing war with them on the state byways. I've been blown into ditches, hit by stones, and threatened with tire irons. So I have a tendency to want to take on trucks personally.

A few years ago, College and I were blown off the road by an 18-wheeler. College flipped over on his bike, and the chain came off. I was livid. I spat the grit out of my mouth and went chasing after the truck, pedaling hard. Behind, I could hear College hollering at me, "Stop, at least wait for me!"

The truck pulled up at a light. I braked and leaped off my bike. Just then a guy stepped out . . . and then another guy got out . . . and then another. The last guy pulled a knife out of his back pocket, just a pocketknife, I noted, but still, it looked ready to unfold. By now, however, I was too angry to be scared.

"Are you trying to kill me?" I asked.

"You don't belong on this road," one of them said.

"What do you mean we don't belong?"

"I pay taxes on this road," another one said.

I burst out laughing. "Yeah, taxes are a hot issue with me, too," I said. Just then, fortunately, College arrived, and stepped between us, and advised me to calm down. We haggled about the tax issue a bit more, and all of us decided to get back to our respective vehicles and move on.

Things like that have happened again and again. Sometimes it's dangerous, and sometimes it's funny, and sometimes it's a little of both. There's a particularly bad stretch of road we call Redneckville, a desolate sector where trucks roar through the intersections and the only businesses for miles are a couple of convenience stores. One morning, I was out riding with another local Austin cyclist over the blacktop when an old pickup truck came right for us. It aimed its windshield toward us and never wavered, a game of chicken. We veered off the road and sailed into a ditch, both of us flying over our handlebars.

We lay there, scraping the dirt off, when we heard a disembodied voice speak to us from above.

A telephone repairman was high on a pole, peering down at us. He'd watched the whole thing. His voice floated down to us from the phone wires.

"If you-all don't call the cops, I'm calling 'em. 'Cause that's not right."

The result of these adventures is that I'm more careful riding my bike around Austin. These days I travel with somebody following me in a car, or on a motorbike, to help shield me from the trucks, the rocks, and the cranks in their pickups. I can't afford to get hit or hurt by some guy coming from behind.

I still like to ride out on isolated roads with friends, though. We ride, and we think aloud, and talk. Once when College and I were out riding, we discussed risk, and recklessness, and the difference between the two. What's adventurous and what's plainly imprudent? To me, what I do on my bike or with my body is not high-risk, because I'm a professional. I have expertise in handling my own limbs, and what might seem risky to others is mundane to me. Chasing truckers, on the other hand, is purely reckless.

"I'm going to give you a hypothetical situation," College said. "You die. Luke has no father."

He was obviously trying to scare me. I was silent.

"And your twins grow up having never really met you."

I thought it over.

"Well, look," I said. "First of all, ain't nobody killing me."

College threw back his head and shouted with laughter. "Lance Armstrong, ladies and gentlemen," he said.

He was right, of course, but I wasn't about to give him the satisfaction. The truth is, I may never be reformed, may never find the proper balance between risk and caution. But I try to be more careful, and my caution grows in direct proportion to the number of people I love, my circle of family and my friends. When I'm descending a mountain, I'm less aggressive than I used to be. In the old days I'd descend so fast, sometimes I'd catch cars. Now I don't need to, I just get down the mountain, because the fact that I have a family is in the back of my mind. You can't win a race on a descent, but you can lose one, and you can lose your life, too. I don't want to lose my life, all I have, on a mountainside.

The real reason I drive a family car now isn't just for the kids. I drive it simply so that I'll slow down.

But some things in me won't change: I like to control things, like to win things, like to take things to the limit. A life spent defensively, worried, is to me a life wasted.

You know when I need to die? When I'm done living. When I can't walk, can't eat, can't see, when I'm a crotchety old bastard, mad at the world. Then I can die.

Maybe I didn't do enough cannonballs when I was a kid, because I was so busy working hard, making my own living and trying to get out of Plano. Or maybe I have a different appreciation of what limits really are. Who knows? Maybe one thing the pitched-back experience does is make the barriers different, one threshold higher. Life, to me, is a series of false limits and my challenge as an athlete is to explore the limits on a bike. It was my challenge as a human being to explore them in a sickbed. Maybe cancer is a challenge no one needs, but it was mine.

All I know is, something makes me want to jump.

So this is about life. Life after cancer. Life after kids. Life after victories. Life after some personal losses. It's about risk, it's about agenda, and it's about balance. It's about teeing the ball up high and hitting it hard while trying not to lose control. And if you shank it, then go and find your ball and try it again . . . because the way you live your life, the perspective you select, is a choice you make every single day when you wake up. It's yours to decide.

My ranch, which I bought with my father-in-law, Dave Richard, is on a bluff near a town called Dripping Springs. I've named the property Mirasol, which means, "to watch the sun." The house will be positioned on the highest point of the 204 acres, and turned at an angle so that it catches the sun as it meanders down in the summer, or as it sinks more hurriedly in winter.

The first time I ever went out to Dead Man's Hole, I traipsed around it with Dave. I studied the waterfall and took a picture of it. Afterward, it stayed with me. I kept looking at the picture, and I showed it to Kik, and I said, "I'm jumping off that sucker." She just said, "Okay."

Finally, I went back out there with Dave and my friend and architect, Ryan Street, who is designing the ranch house. After we did some work sighting the house, we climbed into a truck and drove down through the brush and parked in a grove of live oak. From there we hiked to the swimming hole. First, Ryan and I slid into the pool and checked its depth. Ryan dove down deep and came up sputtering. He said, "I went down until my ears rang," he said.

"Maybe you should go deeper," I said uncertainly.

"I'd get the bends," he said.

We climbed back up, and then stepped carefully through the rocks, looking for a good place to jump from. Finally we found the spot we were looking for. I stood there, shaky in my knees, with that parchedness in the roof of my mouth.

"Don't touch me," I said to Ryan.

"I'm nowhere near you," he said.

Knees bent, I peered over the edge. "Oh, man," I said.

Down below, I saw Dave sitting on a fallen tree by the pool. I yelled at him over the noise of the waterfall.

"Hey!" I hollered. "Why aren't you jumping?"

"I qualify for Social Security next year," he yelled back. "I don't want to screw it up!"

I laughed at that. And then I straightened up, and I jumped. I fell, and fell some more. My arms started to pinwheel, until I remembered to gather them in and hold them tight to my body. When my sneakers hit the water, it sounded like cement breaking.

I came up laughing. I could hear Dave applauding and cheering from the side of the pond. I climbed out, and we toweled off, and then we hiked back up the ridge. We strolled to a small creek where there's a dammed-up fishing hole, through a pasture of waving rye grass, the kind that used to brush against the bellies of horses as they made their way. We paused there and I scanned the pond, looking for fish.

While I stood there on a rock, I saw a pure red dragonfly, the reddest-winged bug I'd ever seen. And then here came a blue dragonfly, right next to it. I marveled at the two vivid creatures buzzing around each other. "Where's the white one?" I wondered aloud. And then for the fun of it, I burst out singing the national anthem at the top of my lungs, my voice banging off the walls of the little wash.

I was stupidly happy, as if I had a new skin. The scare of Dead Man's Hole made me feel fresh. It was a freshness put there by fear—cleansing, clarifying, sharpening fear. Fear that opened the senses, and brought everything into clearer view. Like I say, a little fear is good for you—assuming you can swim.

But not everyone approved of my pulse-checking methods, especially my friend Bill Stapleton, who also happens to be my lawyer and agent and therefore has a certain interest in my future and all. When he heard I'd made the leap into Dead Man's Hole, he grimaced, and delivered a lecture on how foolish it was, and how I could break something or tear something. But even as he was talking, Bill knew it was useless. "I'm doing it again," I said. Bill knew I was serious, because he knows something else about me, too. He knows I need the action.

"That's great, that's just great," he says. "Why don't you make it the stuff of legend?"

CHAPTER 2

A Regular Guy

I'm just a regular guy. A regular, hardworking, T-shirt-wearing guy. A regular, hardworking, motivated, complicated, occasionally pissed-off, T-shirt guy.

There are some obvious contradictions in that statement, I know. I can't promise to resolve them: even if I could dismantle my psyche, and explain all the neuron-firings of my brain, and the subsequent messages to my muscles and from there to my ventricles, I'm not sure it makes a worthwhile map. Self-examination has not always been my strength; for one thing, it takes too long, and for another, I have the suspicion that it's the old secrets in me, the cheats and slights of childhood, all melted down into one purpose, that make me turn the wheels.

Meanwhile, people hopefully understand that beneath the competitiveness I'm a more sensitive sort than I seem at times, and when I say something like "So?" what it really means is, "I care more than I let on." But it may get wearying doing the work of interpreting me.

We only have inklings as to why we are the way we are. Which parts of any of us are made, which parts self-made, and which parts born? The question isn't an easy one to answer, and we can't answer it solely; we define ourselves in our relations to other people: parents, mates, adversaries, bosses, kids. What surviving cancer teaches you is the magnitude of your dependence on others, not just for self-definition, but for your mere existence. Cancer robs you of your independence; you're reliant on friends, family, and complete strangers, stoic doctors and nurses, and when you finally recover, you're never casual again about your place in the human chain.

Sometimes we define ourselves through people we don't even know. That was the case with Sally Reed and me; without cancer there would have been no likely connection between a bike rider and a fiftysomething woman who, as she jokingly puts it, would have otherwise spent most of her time watching daytime TV. We were strangers in the spring of 1999, but our paths crossed due to what Sally calls a "universe wink": I was en route to winning my first Tour de France when Sally was diagnosed with cancer. The day after Sally's first chemo treatment, a friend told her to tune in and watch me ride in the Tour, because I had made an amazing return from the disease.

I had just launched the Lance Armstrong Foundation, and a volunteer there who knew Sally asked me if I'd sign a poster for a nice lady who lived in the Austin suburbs and who was fighting a tough case of breast cancer. So I did.

"Be brave, and fight like hell," I wrote to her.

Sally put the poster up in her kitchen, and she looked at it every day as she endured six months of radiation and chemotherapy treatments. When she finally finished radiation in December of '99, she began to volunteer at the foundation, even though her hair hadn't grown back yet. She came in without fail every Tuesday and Thursday, driving an hour each way, to answer mail and requests from cancer patients all over the world. She became the most devoted volunteer in the office, dispensing information, advice, and sympathy.

The peculiar thing was, for the longest time we never met face to face. I heard all about her and she heard all about me, but we kept missing each other. I usually went to the foundation on Wednesdays or Fridays, and she was never there. After a while, Sally started joking that I didn't really exist. Once, she left a copy of *It's Not About the Bike* for me to sign, along with a note: "I'm leaving this book but I'm not sure there's an author."

Sally started a Lance Sighting Chart on a big eraser-board in the volunteer room at the center. She made columns for the date, place, and time of each Lance Sighting. One column said, WITNESS OF SIGHTING. The next column said, VERIFICATION OF SIGHTING. And so on. It became a running cause of hilarity in the foundation.

The board filled up with Lance Sightings; all the volunteers marked their columns each time I stopped by. But Sally and I continued to miss each other. She liked to joke that even the delivery man had made a Lance Armstrong sighting, but she never had. One afternoon, her husband saw me out training on my bike. Sally started a new category: SIGHTINGS BY PROXY.

Finally, after about a year of this, I went by the foundation and wrote a note and stuck it in her mailbox. "I am here," I said. "Where are you?" I added, scribbling, "When they let me stop traveling, then you'll have a sighting. In November and December I have no travel, and we'll hook up then."

Sally put a new column up on the board: LANCE LETTER SIGHTING.

About a month later, I got back to town, and I went over to the foundation office. I burst through the door, yelling, "Where's Sally?"

And there she was. She had spent a thousand hours at the foundation before we finally met face to face. We hugged, and liked each other instantly. She was as sweet-faced and good-natured as I'd expected, but there was also an interesting hint of no-nonsense about her. She was a well-to-do wife and mother whose life had been derailed by breast cancer not once, but three times; both of her sisters had also been diagnosed with it. We visited for a while, talking about the foundation a little bit, about how to make people feel strong. And we talked about cars, because we both liked fast ones.

But we've never really talked about cancer itself, and I can't quite say why. Maybe we simply have a kind of telepathy about it. Or maybe we're accustomed to being alone in our thoughts about it, since relatively few of the people in our lives can fully understand the experience. Or maybe we simply choose not to dwell on the horrors of it. What's important is the connection; and through Sally I connect with others, too. She forwards correspondence and special requests from all kinds of people in the cancer kinship, and she sets up encounters between us. What we both understand is that it's a source of strength to someone diagnosed to know someone who has survived. Shared experience makes people feel strong. Sally says that if we can give one patient even five minutes of hope, "then we've done the most important thing."

Sometimes it's the absence of a person that complicates the question of who we are. In my case, I never knew my own father. Eddie Gunderson might as well have been an anonymous DNA donor; he left my mother shortly after I was born, and he surrendered all legal parental rights to her. My mother and I never discussed him. I read in a newspaper story that he once tried to contact me after the 1999 Tour, but I didn't welcome it, and found that I didn't have any interest in knowing him, or in dwelling on him, either. That price was paid. He was the keeper of the secret, the man with the answer to the unanswerable. I intended to investigate the meanings of family through my own children—by looking ahead, not back.

Sometimes one person can be all you need, and that was the case with my mother. She managed to be two parents and a best friend, packed into one 5-foot-3 person, although it wasn't easy. "You were a survivor even before you had cancer," she says. If that's true, it's because of her; she supported us on a secretary's salary, and she was always looking for a way to make our lives better. "If anything is going to get done, you've got to do it," she'd tell me. Plano was a wealthy suburb, and other families had a lot of things compared to us. Whatever we wanted to buy, we had to earn. I didn't have a whole lot of anything—but thanks to my mother, I had enough.

Now that I'm a father, I understand how much she must have wanted to give me. I also understand the hundred small anxious moments I must have caused her—there was always some childhood injury to nurse, from my various bike wrecks and stunts. She laughs at the way I worry over and indulge my own kids. "I'm seeing a side of my son I've never seen," she says. She also wonders if, now that I'm a father, I'll be more inclined to examine the past, and I wonder the same.

I've never wanted to look over my shoulder. Occasionally, friends asked me why I wasn't more curious about the past. "I don't like going backwards," I said. "It just creates a headache." Looking backwards went against my nature; I did my self-seeking on a bike, facing front, at high speed. What I knew how to do best was move forward.

When I was young, I rode to amount to something. Then, later, I rode to prove I could survive, and to astonish all the skeptics who'd left me for dead. But what would be the motive now? What would keep me in the saddle in the fifth and sixth hour, when the snow turned black? That was the question I'd confront in the 2000 Tour de France. I had every intention of winning the Tour again. It never occurred to me to rest on my past victory. An athlete doesn't particularly want a past; that means he's done. He only wants a present and a future.

I know this much about myself: the surest way to get me to do something is to tell me I can't. Explain to me that I can't possibly win the Tour de France again, and I have no choice but to try to win the Tour de France again. That winter and spring, most people doubted whether I was capable of it, for various reasons. The rewards of winning the Tour had ruined more than one rider, made them complacent and killed their careers, and now I knew why.

Generally, one of the hardest things in the world to do is something twice. When you've done it once, there's less reason to do it again, because there are so many other things you might be doing instead. This was truer than I liked to admit. I was struggling to maintain a balance between home, work, training, and commercial endorsements. The days only got busier, not less busy, and I struggled to adjust to new responsibilities, to my family, cancer advocacy, cycling, and endorsements. Whenever I overcommitted to any one of them, I seemed to be neglecting something else, especially Kik and Luke. None of this was to mention routine errands, and business headaches, traffic jams, the daily work of living that could clutter up a day, and obscure that sparkling awareness I thought was mine.

I knew I was dividing my energies too many different ways one afternoon, when I found myself on a golf course, trying to play nine holes and relax. As I was lining up a putt, I held a cell phone to my ear, trying to handle a business matter involving new cycling tires. "Hold on," I said. I put the phone down in the grass, hastily missed the putt, and then resumed the conversation.

On another day, I found myself sprinting through the Orlando airport, pouring sweat, with my bike in a cardboard box, as I tried to make a flight to New York for a business meeting. I was thinking maybe I could get in a couple of hours riding in Central Park. In the end I had to ditch the bike at the airport, because I was so late for the flight. I dropped into my seat drenched, after arguing my way past a stewardess. *This has to stop*, I thought.

In its own way, too much success could deaden you, I realized. I preferred the immediacy of simply trying to stay well, be a good parent, and ride a bike. I didn't want to get too distracted by opportunities and obligations.

I went to my friend Lee Walker, and we had a talk about trade-offs, how to juggle commitments without cheating myself or the people around me. Lee helped me understand that a schedule was not a trivial thing.

"Schedule," Lee likes to say, "is how we make our intentions manifest in the world."

I knew Lee Walker the way everybody around town knew Lee. He was one of the town's more indelible characters, a former president of Dell Computer who had walked away from it all and now ambled around in a pair of worn jeans, old sneakers, and a wide-

brimmed hat, giving away money and good advice. Lee had spent
every day in a suit and tie until he awoke one morning with a sear-
ing pain in his back, from spinal meningitis. While he was ill, he realized he hated his life, and half-hoped the illness would kill him.

After he got well, he started a second life. He left Dell, sold his big
house in West Austin, got a new job teaching at the University of
Texas. He lived near campus in a pretty old house with a wild garden,
and a cottage-office out back with a huge blackboard and bookshelves
to the ceiling. He was a benefactor to a lot of causes and young people
in Austin, including me.

When I first knew Lee, pre-cancer, we talked mostly about money. It was my primary topic; I wanted to learn at the knee of a
fortune-making wizard. I'd print out my portfolio so he could look it
over and advise me. "What are you holding that shit stock for?" he'd
ask. We'd talk about what I was selling, why I was buying, real down-
and-dirty stuff. Happiness to me was making money and acquiring
stuff.

But whatever I imagined happiness to be, pretty soon I wore it
out, took it for granted, or threw it away. A portfolio, a Porsche,
these things were important to me. So was my hair. Then I lost
them, including the hair. Sold the car, dropped a good deal of
money, and barely hung on to my life. Happiness became waking
up.

After that, everything changed between me and Lee. We never
talked about money anymore, except in a theoretical sense, as we'd
both come to understand it: wealth couldn't equal health. We talked
about our pitched-back experiences, and about the basic riddle of
survivorship: how do you hold on to the lessons of mortal illness and

yet still resume your ordinary life, with all of its mundane duties? Lee liked to quote the poet Mary Oliver. "What will you do with your wild and precious self?"

Now, as a Tour champion and a cancer activist, I had too many confusing new choices and roles. Lee persuaded me that the important issue was not money, but time. I began to ask, what did I really want? I wanted to make money, sure, but I didn't want to be exhausted by it, or worried about brand strategies. I didn't want to see my face on a cardboard cutout at a convenience store, and I didn't want to make a movie with Tweety Bird. "I don't think you want to maximize your wealth; I think you want to maximize your name," Lee said. I settled on a few meaningful endorsements and tried to remember that my pressures were a privilege, and that they came with a rare dose of public goodwill. On balance, I just hoped to stick to what I cared about and believed in, without letting it slip personally or professionally.

Meanwhile, everyone in cycling watched and wondered what the wealth, endorsements, and publicity maelstrom would do to me. Miguel Indurain, the great Spanish cyclist, said, "Every rider who wins has the same problem. It changes life forever." *USA Today* printed a story about my endorsements, and called me Lance Inc. The French newspaper *L'Equipe* reprinted it, with a commentary in italics, suggesting I'd spent too much time making money and not enough training.

Most of my opponents in the cycling world regarded the '99 Tour as a fluke—a sensational fluke, but a fluke. The cycling world had refused to believe in me in the first place, and now they suggested that a second victory was implausible. But they did me a favor when they wrote me off, because they gave me my new motive. That, alone, made me want to win another one.

As the skepticism grew, the 2000 Tour became a hugely important race to me, perhaps more important even than '99. Anything less than another Tour title was, to me, a failure. "Watch," I told my friends. "I'm going to win it again. And you know why? Because none of them think I can."

I began *looking* for reasons to be aggravated on the bike; I catalogued each expression of skepticism, every disbelieving remark or expression of uncertainty by an opponent, and used them to challenge myself. I kept a list. It was an old competitive habit that went back to my childhood in Plano, when I'd never had as much money as the other kids, or played the right sport. (They didn't force you to play football in Texas, but they sure wanted you to.) I didn't have the right conventional parents, either. I'd always been underestimated, and I knew how to put it to good use. I thrived on long odds.

"I'm just a regular guy," I said that winter. "And I'll show you what a regular guy can do."

The first thing I did in trying to defend the Tour de France, though, was nearly kill myself.

The world is full of people who are trying to purchase self-confidence, or manufacture it, or who simply posture it. But you can't fake confidence, you have to earn it, and if you ask me, the only way to do that is work. You have to do the work, and that's how the 2000 campaign started, with backbreaking work.

In early May, the U.S. Postal team went into the Alps and Pyrenees for a series of labor-intensive training camps, the idea being that if I rehearsed the pain, punished my body enough and did enough work, maybe it wouldn't hurt so bad during the Tour itself. We traced the routes we'd ride in the Tour, scouting the stages.

The 87th annual edition of the race would cover 2,274 miles and 23 days, counterclockwise around France. It was an admittedly illogical undertaking, but then, the Tour evolved from a bizarre stunt in the first place: in the early dawn of the Industrial Age, a French newspaper offered a cash prize to any fool who could beat other fools in an attempt to circle the country on a bicycle. From the outset the event was plagued by cheating, accidents, and absurdities. Since then, however, it has grown into a full-fledged sport, and a beloved national ceremony.

Bike racing is a peculiar sport by American standards, with a strange ethic and an intricate code, and there are as many unwritten rules as there are written ones. It's actually a high-speed chess match on bikes, and reconnoitering the route was important.

The various members of the U.S. Postal team had different roles along the way. Some of them, like my close friend Kevin Livingston, were strong climbers and it would be their job to help me through the mountains, riding in front to shield me from the wind, and pace me up the climbs, while others, such as my great friend George Hincapie, would help me sprint through the flats. Most of my teammates, like Hincapie, Tyler Hamilton, and Viacheslav Ekimov of Russia, were extremely accomplished riders and very capable of winning big races in their own right, and it was a testament to their dedication that they rode so hard on my behalf. Then there were younger and less accomplished riders who were called "domestiques," whose jobs would be to do everything from ride interference to ferry food and water and equipment to me if I needed it.

Our tactician, or *directeur sportif*, was Johan Bruyneel, a dashing former cyclist from Belgium with a reputation for giant-killing: he'd once won a famous Tour stage by beating Indurain. He is an unexcitable man with steady gray eyes and a cleft chin, and as our director he has enormous patience, a talent for devising race plans, and meticulous attention to details. It was Johan who insisted that we hold those camps and familiarize ourselves with the routes.

We rode for hours on end through the raw European spring. In early May, the weather in the jagged Pyrenees alternated between icy and sun-scorched, and it was on the backside of one of those desolate peaks that I nearly lost the Tour before it started.

We had just climbed a mountain called the Col du Soulour, in order to practice a high-speed descent that might be important. As we went up, the mountain sun baked us. I took my helmet off my sweat-soaked head and hooked it over the handlebars. At the top, I paused while one of our mechanics made some adjustments on my handlebars. Then I pushed off, crouched over the bars, and dived down the mountain—with my helmet still dangling from the handlebars. It was an elementary mistake.

The descent was narrow and winding, with a steep drop into a valley below to my right, and a brick retaining wall to my left. I concentrated on cornering, without losing speed. I rounded corner after corner, enjoying the rhythm . . .

. . . my front tire hit a rock.

It blew.

The handlebars swung crazily, like somebody had wrenched

them out of my hands. When a front tire blows while you're going 40 miles an hour, you can't steer. What seconds before had been a high-performance rubber tire generating a secure centrifugal force was now shredded on top of a flat carbon rim. The bike shuddered wildly, and my front wheel veered toward the brick wall. I thought, *If I just get it straight, maybe I can slow down enough . . .*

The wall came too fast. There was a ditch just in front of it, and my front wheel plunged into it. I catapulted off the bike—and hit the wall head-first. It was as though the daylight suddenly exploded, and the sky cracked in half.

I lay in the ditch, stunned and bleeding. Johan had been driving in a car behind me, and now he came around the corner to see me lying in a pool of blood. I had a deep cut in my jaw, my head was swelling and I was barely conscious. I'd taken the entire impact on my head. Weirdly, I didn't have a scratch on me anywhere else. I didn't even tear my racing jersey.

I heard people running. Then I heard some voices—Johan, and strangers. Two French-Canadian doctors had just happened to be picnicking in the grass near the brick wall, and they'd watched, aghast, as I piled into the wall and fell in a heap.

I tried to sit up. "*Non, non,*" one of them said, and pressed me back down. The other leaped up and ran to their car for some ice, which they put on my head. I was conscious and awake but I couldn't see out of the ditch. I remember overhearing Johan, speaking with the doctors.

"You know," one of them said, "when we saw him, and heard the impact, we expected to walk over and find a dead man."

I passed out, I think. At some point, an ambulance came and

took me down from the mountains to a hospital in Lourdes. It was the first time I'd needed hospitalization since the cancer, and as the doors swung open, I inhaled the scent of medicines and disinfectant, and felt the old, scared, fluttery sensation in my chest.

I took some stitches in my head and my jaw, and they kept me overnight for observation. I didn't sleep. I kept feeling that plastic mattress-cover underneath the sheets, which I managed to soak with perspiration.

The next morning I flew home to Nice. Kik met me at the airport. My head was about three times larger than it should have been, and I had two black and puffed-out eyes, along with scrapes and cuts all over my face. Kik gasped.

"You look like the Elephant Man," she said.

For weeks I sat on the sofa at home, unable to train or race, waiting for my head to regain its normal shape. I had plenty of time to think, and it left me with the conviction that I didn't need to make any more foolish mistakes or take unnecessary chances. I liked descending, and I liked cornering, but now I decided that if I lost 30 seconds, that was okay. I could make it up.

Finally, carefully, I resumed training. The crash had prevented me from making perhaps the most important reconnaissance, of a climb called Hautacam. It was a famed ski station at the top of a mist-shrouded mountain near Lourdes, and it would be the first mountain stage, as well as one of the most difficult.

So I went back. The weather was blustery and I rode the exact route we would take, only there were no spectators and I was alone except for Johan in a follow car. I arrived at the foot of Hautacam, and I began to jog atop the pedals, working my way up the steep hillside. I studied the road as I went, trying to decide where I might at-

tack, and where I'd need to save myself. It was pouring down a mix-
ture of snow and sleet, and my breath streamed out in a white vapor.

After about an hour, I reached the top. Johan pulled up and
stuck his head out of the car window. "Okay, good. Get in the car
and have some hot tea," he said. I hesitated. I was unhappy about
the way I'd ridden.

"I didn't get it," I said.

"What do you mean you didn't get it?"

"I didn't get it. I don't understand the climb."

A mountain could be a complicated thing. I didn't feel like I
knew Hautacam. I'd climbed it, but I was still uncertain about how
to pace myself up it. At the end of a rehearsed climb, I wanted to
feel that I knew the mountain so well that it might help me.

"I don't think I know it," I said. "It's not my friend."

"What's the problem?" he said. "You got it, let's go."

"We're going to have to go back and do it again."

It had taken an hour to get up, and it took about 30 minutes to
get back down. And then I rode it again, straight up for another
hour. This time, at the end of the day, in the driving rain, when I was
done, I felt I'd mastered the climb. At the top, Johan met me with a
raincoat. "I don't believe what I just saw," he said. "All right. Now
let's go home."

That night, I sent my physiological data from the climbs to Chris
Carmichael, my coach. After each day's training session, I studied
the readouts from a small computer mounted on my bike, which told
me my watts, power, cadence, and heart rate. Those figures showed
me where the mountain was hardest for me and where it was easiest.
It was my habit to e-mail the figures to Chris, and he would make
notes and comments and send them back to me.

That night Chris opened the file I sent and looked like at my figures. The next morning, he called me. "It looked like a tough day, seven hours in that weather, but your power was still impressive," he said. "One thing, though. I think the file got corrupted, because the numbers are funny."

"Funny how?" I asked.

"There are two sets of them," he said.

"That's right."

"You did the climb twice?"

"Yeah."

Chris was quiet for a moment.

"You sick fuck," he said.

I started the 2000 Tour with a bull's-eye on my back. At least, that's the way I felt.

The Tour field would be one of the strongest in years, and they were all marking me. It was said that I'd been lucky to win the '99 Tour, because two notable champions had been absent from the field. But now the two former Tour winners, Marco Pantani of Italy and Jan Ullrich of Germany, who had sat out the '99 race for their own reasons, would both be on the start line. The field would be full of champions.

Ullrich was probably the most physically gifted cyclist in the world, a large man who rode with a compelling muscularity, churning big gears. He'd missed the '99 race with injuries and struggled to regain his fitness, but now he was hungry, and a hungry man was dangerous. Pantani, a lean, sharp-featured man with a shaven head over which he liked to wear a piratical scarf, was hungry in a different way. He'd sat out '99 in the wake of a doping scandal and was fighting to regain his standing in the sport community.

The course would be another opponent: it promised three big mountaintop finishes, sweltering heat, dust, mud, sheets of rain. That wasn't to mention the cramped hotel rooms in remote villages.

The race began with a prologue, a 10-mile sprint through a theme-park town, Futuroscope. The prologue was essentially a way of seeding the 200 riders, determining who would ride at the front. The result was a surprise: I finished second to David Millar. Millar was a very good friend of mine and an adventurous young British rider who liked to spend every New Year's Eve in a different country. He beat me by two seconds, with a time of 19 minutes, 3 seconds. When the results were announced over the loudspeaker, David burst into tears. I was disappointed for myself but delighted for him. That night, he slept in the yellow jersey.

We set off on a series of flat, uneventful stages. They were fast-paced and wet; from Tours to Limoges to Dax, we rode in a relentless downpour almost every day. All I needed to do was stay in contention and out of trouble until we got to the mountains.

In the mountains, the real race would begin for some, and end for many. Everything else, by comparison, was jockeying for small advantages and increments. The mountains, according to the French, were "the essence of bike riding and the essence of tragedy." They were where the real separations would occur: when you had one last mountain peak to ascend, the strongest guy would propel himself upward faster. I loved the mountains.

The first mountain stage would take me to Hautacam.

On the morning of the stage, I awoke to a freezing rain. I hopped out of bed and threw back the curtains, and I burst out laughing. "Perfect," I said. It was suffering weather, the kind that could defeat a lot of guys as soon as they got up in the morning. The conditions on Hautacam would be blustery and mist-shrouded, just as they had been when I'd climbed the mountain twice in one day during training. It had been the ideal dress rehearsal.

On the team bus, I told Johan "This is going to be epic."

At the start line you could feel other riders in the peloton dreading the day. They dreaded the pain, and you could feel the fear beat some of them before they ever pushed off. They murmured and hung their heads in the rain and frowned at the weather. I felt ready. I announced to my teammates, "This is a day at the beach. Bring it on."

But that didn't mean it was easy. The terrible rainstorms didn't relent, and a tough Spanish rider named Javier Otxoa surprised the field with a breakaway just 50 kilometers into the ride. He built a huge lead that would last all day. None of us chased him, conserving our energy for the big climbs.

The long day wore on our legs, and my teammates dropped away, one by one. Up to that point they'd served almost like booster rockets, propelling me to the front. Now they were gone, and I was alone, except for a handful of riders from other teams.

As we approached Hautacam, we'd been on the bike for four hours, ridden 119 miles, and climbed two mountain passes. Ahead was the last steep, monstrous climb, of eight and a half miles. It rose at a 7.9 percent gradient—an average of 7.9 feet up for every 100 feet traveled.

I rode with Ullrich, Pantani, and Alex Zulle of Switzerland, who had been the Tour runner-up in '99 and who might have beaten me, some said, if not for an unlucky crash early in the race. Also just ahead of us were Richard Virenque of France, a wildly popular rider to his countrymen, and Fernando Escartín of Spain. All of us were chasing Otxoa.

We reached the foot of Hautacam—and Pantani stood up on his pedals and attacked. He swung to the inside of the road and accelerated. Zulle immediately reacted and went with him . . . and so did I. For a moment I struggled to keep up and thought, *Oh no, I'm toast.* But Zulle tailed off, and I moved in front of him. I settled into a tempo, fast enough to hurt anyone who wanted to keep up.

I checked over my shoulder, and Zulle was gone. Now it was me and Pantani. I had to be careful; it was important to pace myself, because efforts on a mountainside were like gaskets, as Zulle had just proven.

We reached a slope I knew well, Pantani just ahead of me. I thought, *All right, baby, I'm gonna light your ass up right here.* I stood up and drove my feet down on the pedals. My bike leaped ahead of Pantani's. Johan came on the radio and said, "He's hurting. He's coming off your wheel." I glanced back and saw him sliding away behind me. Another moment, and he lost contact with my bike altogether.

I swept up the hill. I hadn't just trained my legs for this push up Hautacam, I'd also trained my expressions. I wanted the other riders to see strength in my attitude on the bike, because there was something dispiriting about watching another rider move past effortlessly while you suffered. The only giveaway to how hard I was working was the flaring of my nostrils.

By the time I crossed the line, I was the leader of the Tour de France. I'd started the day in 16th place, more than six minutes behind, and now I was in first.

Ullrich, Pantani, Virenque, Zulle, and Escartín were all at least seven minutes behind me at the finish. Pantani, down by 10:34, went to his trailer wordlessly and slammed the door. Virenque shook his head and said, "Armstrong came on us like an airplane."

There was one rider faster than me that day though: Otxoa. He had hung on to finish 42 seconds ahead, and was the stage winner. I'd managed to wipe out more than ten minutes of road between us, but I couldn't close the final gap. I wasn't sorry; it was a great, courageous ride by Otxoa, one I applauded. I had what I wanted, the overall lead and the yellow jersey.

It was a good day, a big day, and a day that had perhaps demoralized the other riders. Some said I had blown the race apart. Walter Goodefrot, Ullrich's team manager, said, "If Armstrong has no weak days then he will win in Paris. No one can fight him."

But the race wasn't over. Any of the big mountain stages could crack you, and the others wouldn't give up until we saw Paris. I'd learned not to count on anything, and that night at dinner, I balked when Johan asked if the team wanted some champagne. "If we win in Paris there will be champagne," I said. "Paris is a long way off."

The truth was, I didn't know if I had another solo ride like that in me. Those efforts burned you up inside, and you simply couldn't do too many of them. The other riders knew as much, and they would try to isolate me and wear me out.

The 12th stage was likely to be a decisive one: it was a 93-mile journey to the top of Mont Ventoux, a desolate summit that loomed over Provence about an hour outside of Marseilles. Ventoux was the hardest climb of that year's Tour, or any other: just 14 miles from the finish line we'd be at barely 900 feet above sea level, but by the end we'd be at 6,000 feet. The place didn't look like anything else. It looked more like a moonscape than the mountains. What's more, Mont Ventoux could literally kill you.

Some of the greatest climbing legs ever had been ridden to the summit, but it was also the scene of a tragedy. In 1967, British cyclist Tommy Simpson, riding under a broiling sun, had weaved across the rode and fallen off his bike. Spectators urged him to quit, but he said, "No, put me back on my bike." He got back on, and tried again for the summit, but he collapsed again and died near the peak; later, stimulants were found in his blood. The Ventoux was a dangerous, difficult, haunting climb.

We began the stage by riding into the *mistral*, a powerful north wind that beleaguers the entire region, blowing over our shoulders from the front. We rode for more than three hours until we reached the Ventoux, where the temperature suddenly dropped into the 30s.

The ascent itself would last about 13 miles—through *mistral* gusts of 40 miles per hour to a windswept peak. For the first few miles, Pantani probed, trying to see if he could open a lead. He would surge, and then fall back, and surge, and fall back.

With roughly three miles to go, as we neared a memorial to Tommy Simpson, I stood up and moved past Pantani. As I did, I turned and spoke to him.

"*Vince!*" I said, in my poor Italian.

Meaning, "Come on, come with me."

I meant to urge him on, to invite him to ride with me, because I intended to help him to the finish line as the stage winner. Why? At that moment, I felt Pantani deserved the win. He'd had a long, hard year trying to reestablish his confidence after the drug-testing affair. I thought he was one of the sport's more interesting figures, a swashbuckling sort, in an electric-pink cycling suit, a bandanna, and an earring. That day he'd been behind again and again, and come back. I respected his effort, and it seemed only right that a superb climber like him should win on the Ventoux, especially since I had a ten-minute lead after almost two weeks of racing, and could afford to finish second.

Such a concession is unheard of in other sports, but it wasn't at the Tour. In fact, there could be a strange honor in it. For me, as the overall leader, to win stages I didn't need was an affront to other riders, and potentially harmful to their careers and incomes; they all had incentive clauses, and stage wins were prestigious in and of themselves. Sometimes it was the role of the leader to be a *grand seigneur*—that is, generous. This was something I learned from Indurain, winner of five straight Tours from 1991 to 1995: it wasn't good to win every day. There were 200 riders in the field, all working hard, and each deserved recognition for his efforts, and there were no losers at the end of a day when you had climbed the 10 percent grade up Mont Ventoux at the top of Provence, where a rider had once died making the ascent.

But Pantani misinterpreted me. He thought I said, "*Vitesse*," meaning, "hurry up." It was a matter of interpretation: "*vitesse*" was an insult, as if I was telling him he was riding too slowly, and to get out of my way. He thought I was antagonizing him.

We pedaled side by side toward the finish line, in the fierce wind. I had a choice: I could sprint to try to beat him to the line, or I could choose not to contest the stage, since my overall lead was safe. I didn't contest. A pedal-stroke from the finish, I let up.

All that mattered was that I had widened my lead over my real competition, Jan Ullrich, by another 31 seconds.

But in giving the stage to Pantani, I was doing something that didn't come natural to me. Indurain could give it and people could accept it. But when I did it on the Ventoux, it infuriated Pantani. He felt I'd patronized him.

"When Armstrong told me to speed up I think he was trying to provoke me," he said afterward. "If he thinks it's over, he's wrong."

I was offended in turn—and I answered back. "Unfortunately, he's showing his true colors," I snapped. I also publicly called him Elefantino, a nickname he hated. It referred to the way his prominent ears stuck out from under his bandanna.

That set off a feud that lasted for a week. The next day Pantani bolted to the front and won a mountain stage without my help, and afterward made it plain that he hadn't appreciated my sense of etiquette. "It's much more satisfying to finish alone," he said, pointedly. "There's a different taste of victory when you leave everyone behind. A taste of triumph."

Now I regretted Mont Ventoux, and it ate at me. My friend Eddy Merckx, the great Belgian five-time Tour winner, scolded me. "That was a big mistake," he said. "The strongest rider must always win Ventoux. You *never* make a gift of Ventoux. Who knows if you'll ever have another chance to win it?" I felt I was the strongest rider, but I'd let sentiment get in the way. If I was ever in a position to give Pantani a gift again, I thought, *he ain't getting it.*

Over the next few days I was angry and distracted. Anger, however, is not sustaining; you can't ride on it for long, and in this case, it cost me my good judgment. First, I gave in to sentiment, and then I let a quarrel distract me, and neither served me especially well.

We arrived at the final mountain stage, the last dangerous part of the Tour. It was a comparatively short but difficult ride of 122 miles, to the top of a mountain called Joux-Plane. It was the kind that could lull you; because it wasn't an especially long stage, it was tempting to think the ride wouldn't be as difficult. Wrong. Shorter stages are faster, and therefore sometimes harder.

Pantani went out hard, specifically to bait me—and lured me into one of the worst mistakes of my career. "I wanted to explode the Tour without worrying about the consequences," he admitted later.

The attack put our U.S. Postal Team under pressure, and Johan and I talked back and forth on our radios, discussing strategy. How much should we let Pantani get away? I badly wanted to beat him to the finish this time. The action was intense, and my resentment was very high. For 50 miles Pantani stayed ahead, with me chasing.

But we were riding strong, and I felt good on the bike. So good that I passed my last chance to eat, and spun through a feed zone without a second thought. It was a feeble mistake, an unthinkable one for a professional, but I made it. We were so focused on tactics and on Pantani that I forgot to do the simplest thing. It never occurred to me what the consequences of not eating could be.

Finally, I caught him on the approach to Joux-Plane. There, he began to fall back with stomach pains, and eventually lost 13 minutes. But he had done what he had set out to do: ruin my day.

We hit the foot of Joux-Plane, and I went up hard, drafting behind Kevin Livingston as we climbed. Other riders dropped off, unable to match our pace. It was just us. Then Kevin, worn out, fell back too.

All of a sudden I was alone. And all of a sudden I didn't feel very good. It started with a telltale tiredness in my legs, and then a hollowness in my stomach. I had no water, no food, no protein bars, nothing—and no way to get anything, either.

I could feel the power draining from my body.

Virenque and Ullrich caught up to me . . . and then simply passed me.

At first I tried to stay with them, and push through the pain, but my speed slowed, and then slowed some more.

Soon, it was as if I was sliding backwards down the hill.

Ullrich and Virenque turned around, surprised. I could tell they were thinking, *What's he doing? Is he faking?* Initially, I'd ridden away so easily from them, but now I was in trouble and it was written all over my face.

There were ten kilometers to go, six miles. But it felt like sixty. Johan came on the radio—he could tell exactly what was happening from my slow pace. Johan, as a former cyclist, knew what could happen if a rider broke. His worst fear wasn't that I would lose the lead. It was that I might collapse, or quit altogether, lose the entire race right then and there.

Johan kept his voice casual on the radio, even though he must have felt the pressure. Not only was I bonking, but riding in the car with him as a VIP guest was the prime minister of Belgium. "Don't worry, you have a big lead," he said mildly. "You can afford to give some of it back."

The smart play, Johan advised, was to back down my pace and allow myself to work slowly up the hill, limiting the loss. The worst thing I could do was push harder, because that could mean going to zero, totally empty. And that was when people failed physically and fell over sideways.

Every revolution of the pedals sapped me more, and put my body at a greater deficit. It was a question of fuel, of calories or the lack thereof.

That kind of depletion could make strange things happen. As the body broke down, so did the mind.

You went cross-eyed, or the snow turned black. You hallucinated. You tried to talk through your ears. Or you got off your bike. You coasted to the side of the road and stopped, because you simply could not pedal.

If you got off the bike, you were done, out of the race. And I was not that far from completely stopping.

I'd seen riders lose as much as ten or even 15 minutes in that situation, with a long, hard climb ahead and nothing left. I'd seen them drool. I'd seen them disintegrate, and never be quite the same riders again. Now it was happening to me. Steadily, I deteriorated. It was my darkest day in a race.

I began to lose any sense of where I was, or what I was doing. One of my few rational thoughts was, *A lead of seven and a half minutes is a long time; don't lose all of it.*

Johan kept talking steadily into my ear, saying the same thing. "Just relax, ride your pace, don't push it. You can lose a minute, two minutes, three minutes, four minutes, and you are okay. *Just don't stop.*"

Up at the finish line, Bill Stapleton and a group of friends who'd come over to see me race sat in a VIP luxury trailer. They sipped wine and snacked while they followed the action on TV. At first no one noticed that I seemed to be slowing. But then I fell off the front and began to fade. Ullrich and the others began to put real time on me. Suddenly the noise in the trailer went from happy chatter to confusion. Somebody said, "Oh my God, what's going on?" And then there was silence, just absolute silence.

On the bike, I couldn't think straight anymore. I was so dehydrated that my body temperature went funny. I got the chills. My limbs felt hollow, empty. Empty, empty, empty. A Sunday cyclist on a casual ride could have passed me.

Standing in the crowd on the mountainside watching me labor upward was Bart Knaggs. By this time, there wasn't much that Bart and I hadn't been through together, along with our other great friend, College. As I say, you define yourself partly in relation to other people, and Bart and College had been there for some of my defining moments. They'd sat with me when a doctor gave me a probable death sentence and informed me that even if I lived, I'd crawl out of the hospital. They'd been at my bedside again after brain surgery. Bart and his wife, Barbara, who had twin baby daughters, had been close confidants when Kik and I went through the in-vitro fertilization that made Luke.

Bart, College, and I had ridden together across miles and miles of Texas hill country, laughing and trash-talking, or just talking. I liked to taunt them on the bike, ride even with them for a while, and then light them up. But when we weren't horsing around, we helped each other, too. One day we took an exceptionally long ride to Wimberly and back, over miles of rolling highway. Finally, Bart had enough and pulled off, and took a shortcut home, but College tried to stay with me. He did okay until we got to Dripping Springs, when he hit the wall. His body started salting up, and he got weak. I gave him a Coke, which revived him a little, but that didn't last, so I started screaming at him to get on my wheel, and pulled him for a while. But when we were only about five miles from home, he could barely pedal anymore. He screamed back, "I can't do it," and I screamed, "Yes, you can." Then I started laughing, and I said, "Oh, if you could see yourself now." He was pale, white, and slumped over his handlebars. As we hit the last big hills coming into Austin, I put my hand on his back, and pushed him up the slope toward home.

Not long after that, I got the cancer. I kept trying to ride, though, and Bart and College would go with me. Now they were the ones who could leave me in the dust, because I was so weak. One afternoon, when I was bald and thin and yellow from my third chemo cycle, I wanted to ride. I should have been in bed, resting, but I insisted, so Bart and College went with me. We only went three or four miles when we came to a hill. I started failing. "I can't go on," I said. "I gotta go back."

College reached out and put a hand on my back and pushed me up that hill. I almost cried with the humiliation of it, but I was glad for the help. Those were the things we did for each other. What goes around comes around: we all need a push sometimes. If you're the one pushing others up the hill, there may come a day when you need a push, too. Maybe when you help someone, you're that much closer to the top yourself.

Now here was another defining moment. On Joux-Plane, Bart, who knew me better than anyone, stared at my ashen face and my eyes, which now were red-rimmed and badly bloodshot. He saw how the bike swung unsteadily underneath me, and he knew exactly what had happened.

He couldn't push me up the hill. So he did the next best thing.

He started to run alongside me, screaming encouragement. "Go, go, go, go, go!" he screamed. "You can do this! Don't you stop!"

I didn't acknowledge him. I just stared straight ahead. Bart kept running, uphill, and screaming, "Come on, just get to the top!" Finally, the pitch of the mountainside got the best of him, and he couldn't keep up.

I never really knew he was there. I don't remember even seeing him. All I remember, vaguely, is the sound of his voice. It seemed as if it was lost in static, but it was there. I thought it was coming through my radio.

Now Johan's voice crackled in my ear. Apparently I had gone long minutes without responding to him. I don't know if my radio reception had failed in the mountains, or if I had simply been unconscious on the bike.

"Lance, talk to me," Johan said, crackling through the radio. "Where are you? Why aren't you responding?"

"It's okay," I said.

"You have to talk to me," Johan said.

"It's okay, it's okay," I babbled. "I talked to Bart."

"What?"

"I talked to Bart," I said, woozily.

I was delirious.

I don't know exactly what kept me on the bike, riding, in that state. What makes a guy ride until he's out of his head? I guess because he can. On some level, the cancer still played a part: the illness nearly killed me, and when I returned to cycling, I knew what I'd been through was more difficult than any race. I could always draw from that knowledge, and it felt like power. I was never *really* empty. I had gone through all that, just to quit? No. Uh-uh.

But Bart kept me there, too. If there was any question in my mind of stopping, Bart's voice interfered. I could not have finished the stage alone—and didn't.

Whatever I was as a cyclist was the result of a million partnerships, and entanglements, and any cyclist who genuinely believed he had done it all by himself was destined to be a lonely and losing one. The fact is, life has enough lonely times in store for all of us.

If I had any doubts on that score, they were settled by what happened next. About halfway up Joux-Plane, I got some added, unexpected assistance from two riders who came up behind me, Roberto Conti and Guido Trentin. They were good, strong, respected riders who I was fairly friendly with. They saw immediately what state I was in. What happened next was a classic case of cycling sportsmanship, and one I will never forget: they stayed with me, and helped me to the top. Without being asked, they moved in front, shielding me from the wind, allowing me to draft on them, and sparing me untold amounts of work. It was a gesture typical in the Tour; we were competitors, but we shared a mutual compassion for extreme physical suffering. Without Conti and Trentin, who knows how much time I'd have lost before I got to the top?

Fortunately, the last few miles of the stage were all downhill. Once Bart and my other friends had pulled me to the top of Joux-Plane, I sagged over the handlebars and coasted to the bottom. In the end I lost only 90 seconds off my lead. But I might easily have lost everything, and I knew it.

"I could have lost the entire Tour today," I told the press frankly afterward.

When I saw my friend Jeff Garvey from Austin, I said, "So how'd you like amateur hour at the Tour de France?"

I have very little recollection of anything else I said or did between the time when I first began to suffer, and when I finally crossed the finish line. For instance, Chris Carmichael came over to the hotel and met me in my room.

I said, "Where the hell have you been?"

"What do you mean?" he said. "I was there, right there when you crossed the line."

"You were?"

That night at dinner, I apologized to the entire Postal team. I had nearly wasted the efforts of everyone involved. "I will never, ever do that again," I promised. In retrospect it was a great lesson: the mountains were so unforgiving that in one bad hour, or one bad minute, you could lose it.

The next question was, would I be able to recover? How much had it torn me apart getting up that mountain? It was like driving a car with no oil in it; the potential damage to my body could have undermined the whole transmission, ruined the fitness I'd worked for months to build. Sometimes riders had terrible stomach problems—like Pantani, who had cramps and awoke the next morning unable to race, and dropped out. If I wasn't able to revive myself, I could have another disaster. But to my relief, I felt fine that night, and just wanted some hard sleep.

Back home, Kik had to watch the whole thing on TV, and it was wrenching, because she knew what must be happening and how much I was suffering.

I called home. "Well, that was the worst day I've ever had on a bike," I said. "I almost lost the Tour de France today."

Kik said, "But you didn't."

It was my last doubtful moment. All that remained were the flats, uneventful stages toward Paris, and as we neared the finish, I finally allowed myself to accept that I was the winner. But I wasn't quite satisfied. I wanted to make up for the stage win I'd given away. I still cringed over that.

On July 22, I did what I'd failed to do previously, and finally won a stage, a 36-mile individual time trial between the French and German borders from Fribourg to Mulhouse. I went all-out, as the leader in the traditional yellow jersey should. I wanted to represent the jersey, and to feel like an outright winner. I crossed the line spent. My eyes were glazed, and spit was hanging out of my mouth. When someone asked me a question, I couldn't even respond verbally. I just moved where I was directed. I was barely conscious of what I'd done: I'd won with the second-fastest time in the Tour's 87-year history, in one hour, five minutes and one second, averaging about 33.5 miles per hour.

In Paris, a large Texas flag flew from the Hôtel de Crillon. During that last ride, I finally let myself have champagne, and sipped a glass as we rode along. Finally I crossed the finish line with a time of 92 hours, 33 minutes, and 8 seconds for the 2,270 miles. On the podium, Kik handed me our nine-month-old son, and I raised him up, with tears in my eyes.

Ullrich was a generous runner-up. "Armstrong earned it," he said. "He met our every attack." It meant a great deal after all the remarks by other cyclists who said I couldn't repeat. You could field a whole team with the people who thought they could win the Tour and beat me. *Well, they're all here now*, I thought. But it wasn't about revenge anymore; I'd left my taste for revenge on Joux-Plane. There comes a time in every race when a competitor meets the real opponent, and understands that it's himself.

That night, we had a huge victory dinner at the Musée d'Orsay, in a private ballroom with a frescoed ceiling. There were hundreds of people there, including about 80 who had flown in from Austin. Finally I stood up and spoke to my teammates. The reason we were celebrating, I said, was because we had worked harder than anyone else, and the result was that we were no longer the long shots, the flukes; we were established champions. "I feel like we know how to do this now," I said. "We learned how to do it, and now we can do it again and again."

I no longer viewed my cycling career as a one-time comeback. I viewed it as confirmation, and continuation of what I'd done in surviving cancer. But in repeating the victory, I made a pleasant discovery: no two experiences are alike. Each was like a fingerprint, fine and distinct.

How were they different? I'd suffered more in winning the Tour a second time, experienced more physically taxing moments. I could tell that from the thinness of my neck, and the way my ribs and shoulder blades jutted out of my shirt. But in a way, suffering made it more gratifying.

Suffering, I was beginning to think, was essential to a good life, and as inextricable from such a life as bliss. It's a great enhancer. It might last a minute, or a month, but eventually it subsides, and when it does, something else takes its place, and maybe that thing is a greater space. For happiness. Each time I encountered suffering, I believed that I grew, and further defined my capacities—not just my physical ones, but my interior ones as well, for contentment, friendship, or any other human experience.

The real reward for pain is this: self-knowledge. If I quit, however, it would have lasted forever, that surrender, even the smallest act of giving up, would have stayed with me for the duration. When you felt like quitting, you had to ask yourself which you would rather live with.

After it was all over, someone gave Bart a picture. It was of me, pale and delirious as I suffered on the climb up Joux-Plane. In the background, Bart is running alongside me, urging me on. Behind Bart is a guy dressed up as the Devil, one of those costumed characters who haunt the roadsides of the Tour and give it a circuslike atmosphere. It was as if they represented the two choices, either to keep on or to quit.

To me, it was a classic photograph of Bart, because that's the kind of friend he is, the kind who is there on your worst day ever. Your very worst, not the glory day. That day, my worst, one of my best friends was right behind me, on foot, screaming at me to keep going. Maybe it was the real victory to have the same people around me, whether it was a day spent in a hospital bed, or a day when I almost lost a race.

Bart signed the picture and gave it to me. "Lance, we've been to a lot of places . . . but let's not go back there again, OK?" he wrote.

I framed it and hung it on my wall.

The Only Easy Day Was Yesterday

Some things you can't win, though I don't like to admit it. I'm not used to losing much of anything, whether it's a race or a debate, but among the things I've nearly lost are my life, my neck, and my good name, and I've gained a realization: a life of unbroken success is not only impossible, it's probably not even good for you.

Some losses are more tolerable than others, and some things are unrecoverable, and the echelons of loss change in crisis. It's surprising what you can let go of, depending on the circumstances. When I need reminding of this, I think of Sally Reed's hair.

When Sally was undergoing cancer treatment that summer of '99, she watched me ride in the Tour de France. She was in bed, sick and exhausted for an entire week after an infusion of chemo, but she'd turn the TV on and follow the stages, as I rode through the mountains and in the lead of the Tour. She'd go into the bathroom and get sick, and then get in bed again, and watch me ride an alp. Then she'd get up, go into the bathroom and get sick again. "I'd get sick and then come back to the TV to get my hope back up," she says.

I won the race on her 50th birthday. On the morning that I crossed the finish line in Paris, she was 50, and losing all of her hair. It was falling out in handfuls. But because I had won the Tour, she didn't mind the loss anymore. She was so full of . . . *something* . . . that she didn't care. Instead, she and her daughter went out on the deck, and as the breeze blew the loose strands of her thinning hair around her face, she stood there and gently pulled the rest of her hair away. She turned and threw the strands into the wind.

"Let the birds make nests out of it," she said.

Any temptation I have to brood over losses is tempered by the knowledge that I can afford to lose just about anything, except my life and the lives of the people I care for. The less-than-excellent season of 2000–2001 would include losses, both on and off the bike, but it would have been immeasurably harder without that context. Like Sally says, my house is burned, but I can see the sky.

That year saw the beginning of a long, hard defense of my character. I'm surely the most drug-tested man on the planet. I'm tested anywhere from 30 to 40 times a year, both in and out of competition, and I welcome it, because frankly, it's the only proof I have of my innocence.

How do you prove a negative? All I can do is to submit to the endless needles and cups, no matter what the time of day or how disrupting to my private life. Innocence is something I've had to declare and demonstrate on an almost daily basis, and not always successfully, either. "Doper," the French scream at me. That's okay. I have an easy heart.

I've never once failed a test. Not one. Nor do I intend to, ever. You know why? Because the only thing you'll find evidence of is hard work, and there's no test for that.

But no matter how many tests I took, there were still those who considered me guilty, a doper-mastermind who outwitted scientific communities across the globe, and the suspicion reached a height in 2000–2001.

For a while some people even believed I was given a miracle drug during chemo. Reporters used to call my oncologist, Dr. Craig Nichols, and grill him about what he had done to me: exactly what medications had I taken, and what were their effects?

Finally, one day, while yet another reporter was interrogating him as to how he had Frankensteined me, Dr. Nichols wearied of all the questions.

"I put in a third lung during surgery," he said.

He waited for laughter. But there was none.

Dr. Nichols decided that much of the skepticism was based on disbelief that someone could not just survive cancer, but prosper. Most people thought if you had it, you were going to die, and even if you survived the treatment, it was inconceivable that you didn't come out a cripple. But I challenged that assumption by returning to a full, productive life. I had behaved, Nichols said, "as if death was an option."

"The treatment is very rigorous," Dr. Nichols said. "There are some risks."

"Such as?"

"Well, something as simple as an infection could become life-threatening."

"You can't kill me," I said.

"I assure you I can."

In some ways, fighting cancer and winning bike races were much simpler, more direct confrontations than the ones ahead in the coming months. How do you fight an invisible opponent like suspicion? You can't; but that sort of acceptance doesn't come easily to any of us, and sometimes the hardest thing in the world to do is . . . nothing.

How do you learn to cope with doubt, and, more important, self-doubt? And how do you learn how to lose?

Trouble is, you're going to lose more than you're going to win, no matter who you are. Most of us overreact when we lose, and over-celebrate when we win, and I'm no exception. I have a love-hate relationship with losing: it makes me brooding and quarrelsome. But the fact is, a loss is its own inevitable lesson, and it can be just as valuable as a victory in the range of experiences, if you'll examine it.

When you ride a bike for a living, you see a lot of stuff, and after a while you understand that the races aren't really races but expressions of human behavior; and that behavior can be brave, fraudulent, funny, seeking, uplifting, and downright parasitical. Some of what you see you like, and some of it you don't like very much, and it's all very interesting, and telling, but it ain't war and it ain't death and it ain't childbirth, either, and what losing does is, it restores the perspective.

In August of 2000, I had yet another crackup on my bike. In Italy they say a cat has 12 or 13 lives, instead of nine. I must be an Italian cat, because it was my second life-threatening crash in a year.

I was out on a training ride in the hills above Nice with my Postal teammates Frankie Andreu and Tyler Hamilton, just a cruise to get our legs back after the Tour and begin preparing for the Olympics in Sydney, Australia.

A single lane ribboned up into the mountains above the city, and we followed it until it grew so narrow it didn't have a center line. It was remote, which was why we chose it: you could ride it for hours and not see a single car. It was purely a chance deal that one ran straight into me.

We whirled around a blind left-hand curve, me in the lead. Meantime, a French couple in their car sped into the curve from the opposite direction—and halfway around the turn, we piled into each other head-on. Behind me, Tyler swerved into a ditch. Frankie managed to steer clear.

There was a metallic clap, and my bike disintegrated. I sailed into the air over the hood of the car.

Frankie watched the wreckage of my bike as it clattered along the asphalt, a heap of broken and twisted metal tubes, a couple of them with Trek stickers.

I lay on the ground, dazed. Slowly, I sat up. I stared at the pieces of my bike. The frame itself was in three pieces, the fork was in two pieces, and the wheels were everywhere. The rear part of the bike had been torn from the chain, which was snapped in two.

I wondered if my arms and legs were in similar condition, and began a mental checklist of my body parts. My shoulder and neck hurt, bad. I glanced down and saw my helmet lying next to me. It was cracked in half like a walnut.

I moved a little, and felt an incredible stabbing pain in my back. It was as if a bone was trying to poke through my skin.

"Frankie, look at my back," I said. "Is anything sticking out?"

"No, there's nothing sticking out."

"It's got to be sticking out. I can feel it."

Suddenly, I felt like lying down again. "Unnhhhhh," I said, and fell back on the tarmac.

A Frenchman had gotten out of the car, and now he started

yelling at us. Frankie and Tyler asked him for help, but it quickly became clear he wasn't going to do anything but yell. Frankie and Tyler tried their cell phones, but the reception was lousy in the mountains and they couldn't get through. They eyed the Frenchman. He wasn't going to let us use his cell phone to call somebody, either.

Frankie and Tyler squatted in the dirt next to me, and the three of us conferred. We decided Tyler should ride down the mountain, until he either found help or until his cell phone worked and he could call Kik to come get us.

Tyler rode off, and as I lay back down in the road, something occurred to me.

"Frankie," I said, "slide me out of this road, so I don't get run over."

Frankie and I just sat there. To tell you how remote the road was, we didn't see another car for the next two hours—and then it was Kik's. That's how desolate the road was, and how unlucky we were.

Meanwhile, Kik was experiencing her own drama. Tyler finally got through to her and explained what had happened, but she couldn't hear well enough to make out the name of the village closest to us. The phone connection started breaking up. Kik heard, "We're in (crackling noise), a place called (crackling noise)." Then the phone went dead.

Kik opened a map and stared at the tiny printed names of villages, trying to find one that sounded sort of like what she had heard. Finally, she saw it, and jabbed a pen at it.

She grabbed her keys and raced to a taxi stand, and found a driver we'd gotten to know, and asked if he would show her the way. He jumped in his car, and they took off, winding through the mountains. Finally, after about an hour and a half, they found us.

We were still sitting by the side of the road when Kik pulled up. She did a good job of seeming calm as she surveyed the wreckage, and loaded me and the remnants of my bike into the car.

As we drove down the mountain she asked, "Where does it hurt?" I said, "Right where my back meets my neck."

Kik drove me straight to a local hospital for an X ray—but it didn't show anything. "It's just strained," the doctor told me. I said to Kik, "That can't be right," but I went home and took some aspirin and waited for the pain to go away. Instead it got worse.

I went to a chiropractor, thinking maybe my back was out of alignment, but as soon as he touched me it felt like my spine was breaking in half. As I lay on the table, I began to cry. I couldn't remember the last time I'd cried because something hurt—I must have been a boy. That did it; I went back to a hospital, this time a modern clinic in Monaco, for a CT scan.

The doctor said, "You've got a big problem here." There on the screen was an unmistakable crack, and he explained that I'd fractured the C-7 vertebra of my spine, the link between my back and my neck.

"What's that mean?" I said.

"Your neck is broken."

I had no trouble believing it, after all that pain. I asked what it meant for my cycling. I explained that I planned to ride in the 2000 Olympics and was about to start my most important training. How long would I be off the bike? Would I be able to ride in Sydney?

The doctor looked at me skeptically. "You better think long and hard about that," he said. "I wouldn't advise it. You just won the Tour, what do you need the Olympics for? And if you fall on this injury again, it could be devastating."

He explained the risks: it might be weeks before I regained range of motion in my neck and was able to fully turn my head. Without peripheral vision, all kinds of crashes could occur. It would be a day-to-day thing whether I'd be healthy enough to train, and even then, he didn't think I should risk it. I told him I'd consider what he'd said, and went home to rest.

I had a decision to make. To me, it wasn't a hard one: if I could ride, I was going. Crashes were unavoidable in cycling, and so was bad luck, and if you worried about falling off the bike, you'd never get on. I simply couldn't pass up the Olympics; they were too meaningful. I could win six Tours, and yet if I lost the Olympic gold medal, people would say, "What's wrong with this guy? I thought he was supposed to be a good cyclist."

They were personally meaningful, too. So far, the Olympics represented nothing but failure and loss to me, and I wanted to change that. I hadn't competed well in them in two tries.

I rode miserably as an inexperienced hothead in the 1992 Barcelona Games. I'd gone into the Atlanta Games in 1996 as an American favorite, but I rode disappointingly and finished out of the medals again, 6th in the time trial and 12th in the road race. It felt like I was dragging a manhole cover. I assumed it was the result of nerves, or because I hadn't trained right, but shortly afterward I was diagnosed: it turned out I'd ridden with a dozen lung tumors. Cancer had cheated me out of a chance to win an Olympic medal on native soil.

There was an additional motive for going to Sydney. The Games would end on October 2, an important anniversary, four years to the day after the initial cancer diagnosis. To be at the Olympics on that day would be another way to kick the disease. Also, the coach of the U.S. team was my close friend Jim Ochowicz, who had sat at my bedside during all of my hospital stays and chemo treatments. It was Jim who, early in my career, shaped me into a champion cyclist, and he was also Luke's godfather. I wanted to ride for him again, and I wanted to celebrate the cancer anniversary at the Olympics, with a gold medal as the centerpiece.

After a couple of weeks, my neck was still stiff but getting better, and I was able to ride, so I began training. Meanwhile, some prominent track stars dropped out of the Games, and there were suggestions in the press that they'd done so to avoid drug testing. I began to get calls from reporters, wondering if I would show up in Sydney. The implication was clear: a no-show would suggest that I had something to hide. What no one knew was how hectically I was trying to train to get there.

I arrived in Sydney, thrilled to see Australia for the first time. I felt I was in decent shape, and I still had every expectation of winning: to me, there was no other real reason to be there. I'd been to the Games twice before and come home without a medal—and I wasn't in Sydney for a vacation, much as I loved the Australian scenery.

The first event was a 148-mile road race, and it would be the more difficult of my two events. The course was a long, flat one that didn't especially favor our U.S. team, because there were no hard climbs on which to separate from other riders, which meant a pack finish. The winner would have to fight through a dense crowd of riders, and the field included Jan Ullrich and his German team.

Nothing went right, from the start. Our team was plagued by problems with our radios, and they went out at a crucial moment when we needed to communicate, screwing up our tactics. For a good portion I didn't know where Ullrich was on the course. I thought he was behind me, so I bided my time, pacing myself. Late in the race I pulled up to my great friend and teammate George Hincapie, thinking that a big surge could win it.

"George, George, is anybody away?" I asked.

"No," he said.

I got ready to make my final push. Then we passed one of the big Jumbotron monitors out on the course. It showed Ullrich—pulling for the finish line. It turned out he was in front of me—way in front. He had gotten away from me and I never even knew it.

"George, who's that?" I asked.

Ullrich sailed across the finish line for the gold, while I faded and crossed the finish line in 13th place. I had to laugh at the mishap. I wasn't too disappointed, because we had been an outside shot at the medals to begin with. It was in the next event, the time trial, that I had the best, most realistic shot at a gold medal.

The 29-mile course snaked through the streets of Sydney and finished at a historic old cricket ground. Time trials were my strength; they required a rider to be as precise and technical as he was fast, and I'd won four of them over the last two years to claim Tour de France stages.

But again things just didn't go quite right. There was no huge breakdown, just some minor slippage in form that cost me. After the first lap, I was a second off the lead pace, and the gap just widened from there. By the end of the second lap, I was six seconds down and clearly out of the running for the gold.

I finished more than a half a minute behind the winner, Viacheslav Ekimov.

There was some consolation: Eki was my U.S. Postal teammate and a man I was inordinately fond of and who I deeply respected. Ullrich got the silver medal. I got the bronze.

As upset as I was to lose, I was that happy for Eki. I'd lobbied hard to get him on our Postal team and he'd put it all on the line for me at the Tour, done hours of thankless work while I got the glory. Our friendship and respect was mutual. "Today I'm gold and he's bronze," Eki said. "He understands. Next year we're together."

I'd simply been beaten. I'd gone as hard as I could: my heart rate was pegged at a maximum rate of 190, which told me I'd gone all-out. When you prepare for an event and you do your best and then you don't get it, you just have to say, I didn't deserve to win. Someone was better.

"I felt good," I told the press. "I can't say that I had any major problems. No mechanical problems, no discomfort on the course, no problem with the neck. My preparation was good. I have no excuses. I gave everything and I got third place. The two riders in front of me were better and faster and stronger."

After the medal ceremony I walked past my bike and kissed my family. Kik swore she had never been prouder of me. My mother summed up how she felt to a reporter.

"The thing is, he's just lucky to be here," she said. "Nothing can compare to that fact alone."

But I couldn't see that yet, I was too disappointed in myself. That night, we went out on a boat in Sydney Harbor with several of our closest friends, and as I sat on deck and sipped wine, I felt as if I'd let down everyone who believed in me. I'd asked USA Cycling for a lot: extra bikes, extra mechanics, and special accommodations, and then I didn't win. I stood up and offered a toast, and an apology.

"I just want everyone to know how sorry I am," I said. "I know how much effort you all put into helping me get here, and into being here. I appreciate everything everybody did, and I just want you to know that. I couldn't have gone any harder, any faster. And I'm sorry that I didn't win."

The next day was October 2, and Kik planned a trip for us into the Australian wine country, but by then my disappointment at losing the gold had seeped into me. I tried to enjoy the day, sampling the local wines, as we had lunch on a beautiful terrace overlooking the countryside. But I struggled to make conversation, and by the end of the day I was all but wordless.

The next morning I flew to San Francisco for a long-standing speaking engagement. I was still upset with myself when I landed, and when I called Kik to check in, she could hear it in my voice. Suddenly, she was upset, too.

"You know, I've never been more proud of you than when you lost," she said. "But you just don't get it. You don't get it at all. You're just being moody to everybody around you. You took a perfect day, when we had everything to be thankful for, and you ruined it."

She was right, and I knew it. I apologized, and gave some thought to winning and losing, and how to handle each. When you win, you don't examine it very much, except to congratulate yourself. You can easily, and wrongly, assume it has something to do with your rare qualities as a person. But winning only measures how hard you've worked and how physically talented you are; it doesn't particularly define you beyond those characteristics.

Losing, on the other hand, really does say something about who you are. Among the things it measures are: do you blame others, or do you own the loss? Do you analyze your failure, or just complain about bad luck?

If you're willing to examine failure, and to look not just at your outward physical performance, but your internal workings, too, losing can be valuable. How you behave in those moments can perhaps be more self-defining than winning could ever be. Sometimes losing shows you for who you really are.

The following day I flew home to begin the off-season with an attitude adjustment. Luke took his first steps, and we celebrated his birthday at Chuy's Mexican restaurant. "He told me that's where he wants to eat," I said. Luke scribbled on the menu, crushed tortilla chips all over the floor, and ate quesadillas, while Kik and I had long-awaited margarita swirls.

Kik surprised me by hanging the bronze medal in a place of honor. She continued to insist that it was one of her favorite days. I looked at her like she was crazy.

"My goal was the gold," I said.

"My point exactly," she said.

Maybe the difference between a boy and a grown man, and the difference between a chipped shoulder and nice smooth lines, is the way you handle yourself when you don't get what you want. "I was never prouder," she said, "not for one single second. Not even on the Champs-Elysées in the summers of 1999 or 2000. It was one of the happiest things I've ever seen in my life. Because you wanted that gold medal really bad, and you'd never really tell anyone that. But you wanted it."

She was right about that. "Yeah, but I didn't get it," I said. I'd failed.

"You know what?" she said. "A day will come when Luke will miss the mark, and fail. He will be brokenhearted, and he will think his champion dad will never understand. But there will be this videotape, of a day in Sydney that he was too young to remember, but where an example of how to lose was set. And I'll show it to him, and tell him that I never loved you more."

On Thanksgiving Day of 2000, shortly after I got back from the Olympics, French authorities announced I was under criminal investigation for doping.

I was dumbfounded. I wasn't just being called a cheat, I was being called a felon, under formal investigation.

I picked up the phone and called Bill Stapleton, who was taking a holiday walk in the park with his wife and family. "What the hell is going on?" I said. Bill promised to find out and get back to me. After a while, he called back. "It's ridiculous," he said. "But we're going to have to be patient."

What happened was this: during the Tour, someone surreptitiously videotaped two of our medical staff as they threw away a couple of trash bags. The tape was sent anonymously to a government prosecutor, as well as to the France 3 television station. Now the station was airing the tape while sensationally reporting our "suspicious behavior" as we disposed of "medical waste."

French authorities had responded by launching a full-scale judicial inquiry.

I made some calls, and tried to figure out how we could be in such a situation. According to our team doctor and chiropractor, after a Tour stage in Morzine, they had bagged up the garbage left over from our medical care as they normally did. They didn't want to leave it at the hotel where we had stayed, however, because the more unsavory media was always picking through our garbage in its relentless hunt to prove me a doper, and we resented it. So they decided to frustrate the press by taking it from the hotel in Morzine and throwing it away in a roadside garbage can. This was their "suspicious behavior."

The "medical waste" consisted of some wrappers and cotton swabs and empty boxes, nothing more. In France, as in this country, there are strict rules about how to properly dispose of any serious medical products such as syringes and IV needles. Those had been handled as required, placed in yellow biohazard containers that were picked up by a French medical-waste service.

I immediately issued an angry denial through our Postal spokesman, Dan Osipow. Our team had "zero tolerance" for any form of doping, we said. It sounded like the usual clichéd statement, but we meant it. We were absolutely innocent.

But it quickly became apparent that innocence might not matter. The judicial system in France seemed to be the reverse of American law, with no presumption of innocence, and what little I knew suggested that French legal authorities didn't need much evidence to act. I worried that when I returned to my home in France, they could decide to handcuff me, in front of the world, and haul me off.

Our first concern was to obtain a French lawyer, a gentleman named George Kiejman, and he explained the system to us. There was a *juge d'instruction*, or examining judge, who evaluated evidence and functioned similar to a grand jury in America. This judge, Sophie-Hélène Chateau, had broad subpoena powers.

She promptly subpoenaed all of my urine samples from the 2000 Tour as well as those of the rest of the U.S. Postal team. She appointed an assistant prosecutor, François Franchi, to conduct an investigation. We were charged with suspicion of using doping products, inciting the use of doping products, and using toxic substances.

At first, I tried not to take it personally, and to understand the motives behind the investigation. When an athlete doped, the competitors, spectators, and journalists were defrauded. International cycling had recently been through a drug scandal, and the French were protective of the integrity of the Tour, which was more than just a race, it was a national symbol, and they didn't want it junked up by needles and vials. But I didn't like being accused on no evidence.

Part of the problem, I realized, was a fundamental lack of awareness among the public (and the prosecutors) about just how grueling cycling really is. Medical treatments were an absolute necessity. The Tour de France is not a natural event. We ride more than 100 miles a day for three straight weeks, through incredible and changing conditions. Some cars wouldn't hold up under that physical stress, much less a human body. We needed help, in the form of IVs of vitamins, minerals, and phosphates. You simply can't eat or drink enough to make up for that kind of depletion, to replace all the things you expend.

Those IVs and syringes were health essentials. What's more, every Tour rider suffered cuts, scrapes, and bruises from crashes, not to mention all the assorted rashes, like road rash and seat rash, and then there were the aches, sprains, tendinitis, etc. We were asking something inhuman of our bodies, and we simply couldn't do it without medical assistance.

There was a double standard at work: when a football player got cramps and went to the locker room for a drip, and then returned to the field, everybody called him a hero. But because we were cyclists, we were suspected of doping if we showed a needle and vial.

Suspicion was the permanent state of affairs in the sport, and with reason. Unfortunately, cycling had a long history of doping. It had happened time and again: athletes had lied, had cheated, had stolen. In the 1998 Tour, which I missed while recovering from illness, a drug scandal resulted in multiple arrests and suspensions when a team car was found to be carrying large amounts of the blood-doping agent erythropoietin (EPO). Since then, Tour officials had worked with the International Cycling Union to develop new drug tests, and to restore public confidence in the race.

Drug inspectors arrived at each team hotel between 7 and 9 A.M. on the day that the Tour started and drew blood from the crooks of our arms. After that, there were surprise drug tests—you never knew when someone would bang on your hotel-room door and ask for blood. There were also daily urine tests in a mobile trailer after each stage. (Sometimes there was a long line, so often I would hold my water for the last hours of the stage, to be sure that I had some to give them. At the finish line I would literally leap off my bike and run to the trailer.)

Even out of season, I was, and am, tested by the United States Anti-Doping Agency. It's a moment of wearying familiarity: I'm sitting in my kitchen early one Texas morning in the off-season, sipping coffee and whispering so as not to wake assorted children, when there's a loud ringing at the doorbell. Standing on the front step of my home is a representative from USADA, coming on like John Wayne, holding out a piece of paper like a warrant and telling me to take a drug test, or risk being banned from my sport.

The drug testers in Austin were the same people every time, a husband and wife. I didn't know their names, and wasn't especially cordial with them, because they were never cordial with me. They would ring the bell, I'd open the door, and they would announce, "Random drug control," and hand me a piece of paper instructing me on my rights. Or lack thereof: if I declined the test it was considered an automatic positive, and I would be banned.

What's more, I was required to inform the USADA of my whereabouts at all times. No matter where I went. Anytime I changed locations, I was supposed to fax or e-mail them as to my movements. It was like being under constant surveillance.

But no matter how many tests came back clean, skepticism about my performances persisted, especially in France. The European media had been full of suspicion ever since I won my first Tour in 1999. Throughout that race, some in the French cycling and the French press communities suggested that my victory was too miraculous; that I must be on a drug, and had seized on a technicality and run with it: I used an analgesic cream that contained corticosteroid to treat a case of saddle sores, so the press reported that I tested positive for a banned steroid. It was untrue. I had received permission from race authorities to use the cream, disclosing its contents. In fact, all of my tests were clean, and I asked the Tour to release the results, which they did.

During the 2000 race, skepticism persisted. A headline in *L'Equipe* over my picture had said, sarcastically, LES DEUX VITESSES. "The Two Speeds." The insinuation was clear: that I was riding at a different, unnatural speed.

Hautacam was greeted as a classic climb by some, but to others it was more evidence that I was using some mysterious performance-enhancing drug. Daniel Baal, the president of the French cycling federation (and the man who is scheduled to become the next director of the Tour de France), intimated as much to the press that afternoon after watching me.

"I would love to know what is happening today," he said. "I do not know if we must speak of a new method, or a new substance. I saw many riders in difficulty on the climbs and that is good. But . . . must I have enthusiasm for how the race is being won?"

As much as I tried not to take the investigation personally, I couldn't help resenting it. The French press had made a seamy habit of lurking outside my home in Nice, year-round, even when I was away and Kik was there alone. They smoked, stared at my windows, and engaged in their favorite sport: brazenly picking through my trash in plain view.

Unfortunately, there was no question in my mind that the investigation was launched in part out of anti-American sentiment. The Tour was as French as sunflowers and wine, and I wasn't French. Worse, I was Texan, and only the second American ever to win since the race was founded in 1903. I'd won two consecutive Tours, while native Frenchmen had fared poorly in the race. It was hard not to feel I'd been singled out because I was successful and American. I rode for an American-owned team, on an American-made bike, a Trek. I wore a red, white, and blue Postal uniform, with the flag all over me.

"Why?" I asked my teammate Cédric Vasseur, a Frenchman. "Why are they doing this?"

Cédric said, "In France they don't like the winner. They like the runner-up."

For some reason, the French believed that I, the winner, was doped to the gills—while the guys who got second and third didn't take anything? That didn't make sense. But there it was.

Back in America, the only other American ever to win the race, Greg LeMond, jumped in and began making comments questioning my innocence. He suggested that I was one of the greatest "frauds" in the history of cycling. The investigation, he said, was the French way of guarding the Tour, which he said was more than just a race, it was a beloved French ritual based "on a deep love of the sport."

I snapped back, "Their love of the sport is not greater than mine."

I was mystified and disheartened by the hostility. I loved France, and I wasn't one to say I loved something when I didn't. I was entranced by the beauty of the country and I'd made a part-time home on the Côte d'Azur since 1997. Kik and I had been newlyweds there, and Luke had spent a portion of his first year there. I'd made a life in France, and done so happily. I spent far more time there than in America. I rode in French races to tune up for the Tour, I honored their present and past champions, and I made an effort to learn French and to speak it in public, even though I sounded foolish.

It didn't matter; nothing worked. Michael Specter of *The New Yorker* magazine would eventually write that the French didn't love me for two reasons: they resented that my drug tests were clean when French cyclists had tested positive, and I was too robotic on the bike. French spectators loved the faces of pain going up the mountainside, and there was a whole lore to suffering. They recited certain stories over and over, such as the one about the guy who had to weld his frame together in the 1910 Tour. Those things they never forgot. But I didn't give them enough of those moments; I wasn't expressive, and I very often saw no reason to comment, and I tried to look impassive on the bike.

It wasn't my job to satisfy the French sensibility, to dramatize, to attack in the first kilometer and maybe lose the whole race just to make the French feel good. I loved France, but I didn't love the French press, or the fanatics, and now I didn't love the French bureaucracy, either.

The investigation gathered momentum in December, and so did the press reports. Their focus was a mysterious substance called Actovegin, an empty box of which had been found in our roadside garbage. Almost all of the reports were sensational and erroneous: Actovegin was variously described as an experimental Norwegian medication and as calf's blood, and, according to one especially silly report in the *Times* of London, it had never been used on humans before.

I had never heard of it.

I'd never used it, and to this day I still haven't. On checking, none of my teammates had heard of it, either. Still, the press chattered on: it was a red-blood booster (it wasn't), it was banned (it wasn't), it emulated the effects of the banned erythropoietin (it didn't).

I've since been forced to learn about it. In fact, Actovegin had been around and in use since the 1960s. It was a calf's-blood extract, and there was a good deal of debate in the medical community as to what it was good for, if anything. It was mainly used in European countries to treat diabetes, but it was also used for bad scrapes and cuts, rashes, acne, ulcers, burns, tendinitis, open wounds, eye problems, circulation disorders, and senility. There was nothing to suggest it was performance-enhancing, and it wasn't on anybody's banned list. I want to say that again. It was legal. It was not banned.

Our team doctor had included Actovegin in his medical kit before the race. He kept it on hand because one of our team assistants was diabetic, and also in case of traumatic skin injury—the kind that can happen when you fall off a bicycle onto an asphalt road while traveling at 50 miles per hour.

The head of the French Sports Ministry, Marie-George Buffet, announced that all of our Postal team's urine samples from the 2000

Tour would be turned over to the French judicial investigators and submitted to forensic testing by law enforcement, and so would the garbage that we had thrown away during the 2000 Tour.

That was actually good news. I *wanted* all the tests, because I knew they would come back pure. They were my only means of vindication. "It's the best news in a long time," I said. "Because I know I'm clean."

More good news came when the International Cycling Union announced it would conduct its own tests. The ICU had quietly decided to preserve 91 frozen urine samples taken from the 2000 race, without the cyclists' knowledge, in hopes of eventually submitting them to a brand-new test for EPO.

Prior to that, there was no real way to tell if an athlete was using the drug. EPO is an artificial hormone originally developed for patients on kidney dialysis, but athletes desperate to win had discovered that it could be performance-enhancing, especially in cycling, swimming, rowing, and running. EPO was the most helpful drug to a cyclist because it boosted hemoglobin, allowing more oxygen to flow to the muscles. It was the drug that had caused the 1998 Tour scandal.

The new EPO test could detect whether you had used the substance within the past 72 hours, by testing blood viscosity, counting red blood cells. More red cells make your blood thicker and give you more hemoglobin. The test was designed to compare an athlete's blood viscosity to that of an average person; if the test result exceeded certain parameters, it was considered an indication of EPO use.

The blood-thickening side effect of EPO was considered extremely dangerous in the long term, and some even speculated that it could cause strokes. About two dozen cyclists were suspected of having died from its effects, according to the *New York Times*. Anyone who thought I would go through four cycles of chemo just to risk my life by taking EPO was crazy. It was one thing to seek to maximize performance, or explore a pharmacological gray zone. It was another to court death.

I practiced another, more natural way to oxygenate my blood, and that was to train or live at altitude. I stressed altitude training—it was a big part of my regimen, and it was safe, but it was no fun. It was lung-searing, and dizzying, and inconvenient, but it was legal and it worked.

Here's how: with less oxygen intake, your body becomes more competent and efficient and produces more red blood cells. I went to St. Moritz for a month out of every year to train, and when I wasn't in the mountains, I spent a lot of nights sleeping in an altitude tent.

An altitude tent, as you can imagine, is not the most romantic thing you can bring to a marriage. It's a regular tent, but it's got a device attached to it that's essentially a filter to suction some of the oxygen out of the air to simulate high altitude. I used it in Europe a lot, and I kept one at home that I sometimes used too, though it meant sleeping without Kik, and with a humming machine noise. Sometimes Luke played in it and I'd find it filled with toys and broken goldfish crackers.

One night, Kik and I tried sleeping in it together. Kik said, "This is so romantic, let's go camping."

We lasted about three hours before the alarm went off—signaling serious oxygen depletion. We woke up gasping, and with splitting headaches.

"Sorry," I said. "I didn't know it wasn't meant for two."

"You better get a double," she said.

The vague, distant nature of the investigation in France still frustrated me, but now that there were specific tests, I felt better. If I was a cheater, then it would be apparent when they unfroze the samples I'd given in the 2000 Tour, before the EPO test existed, and when I had no idea they'd been kept and frozen.

Three forensic doctors would conduct tests for French law enforcement. Every drop of my urine and every trace of my blood, and those of my teammates, would be put through exhaustive analysis. Until now, we'd been in a position where we couldn't defend ourselves. But according to the authorities, the tests should be completed by January, and that meant I would be cleared, soon. I looked forward to the big moment: total exoneration.

But it never came. January came and went, with no test results, and the investigators refused to clear me, or to say why.

The winter wore on, uncharacteristically dreary. I called it "the winter of discontent." One setback seemed to follow another. I was beginning to feel harassed: our trash had been picked over, and my blood and urine microscopically examined, and now, the French government started looking at my tax returns as well.

That spring, Johan Bruyneel was ordered to Paris for questioning and found the police station surrounded by press. Every journalist in town was there with a microphone or camera. Inside, he was questioned for three hours. "I felt like a criminal," he said later.

When his interview was finished, Johan asked one of the officers why the investigation was taking so long. Johan said, "All the tests have been done, everything has been done, and there is nothing, nothing, nothing."

The police investigator was sympathetic, almost apologetic. He told Johan, "The scientific expert who does the tests thinks he has overlooked something. He says it's not possible that there is nothing."

Johan was incredulous. "*What?*"

"He says the performance is on such a high level that it's not normal. This guy wants to find something."

So there was our problem. We weren't guilty, but that wasn't necessarily good enough for the French scientist who wanted us to be guilty. All we could do was try to forget about it and go on about our business. But it felt like they were trying to make life difficult in every way they could. Finally, I'd had it. I decided to leave, and I began to scout for a new home, in Spain.

Life in France had in some ways been peaceful, with the Mediterranean pace and the metronomic routine of training, and I'd miss the baguettes, the flowers, the friends, and the view of the mountains against the sea. I'd miss sitting on our terrace and watching the sunsets over the city lights. But I wouldn't miss the trash scavengers and the prosecutors.

Meanwhile, the investigation threatened to seriously mess with my reputation. Bill Stapleton was finding it difficult to conduct business. Coca-Cola was running scared of me, and so were other sponsors.

Bill finally said to them, "Look, he doesn't take drugs, okay? I will stake my entire career on it."

We wrote in anti-drug out-clauses in our contracts: if I tested positive, I'd give the money back.

Bill had also begun trying to negotiate a new four-year deal with the U.S. Postal Service, the contract that was my chief income. But now Postal was wary of re-signing the entire team, and even briefly considered not renewing its team sponsorship. All because of a French fishing expedition. It was hard not to take that personally.

But another, far more personal blow came when Kevin Livingston, one of my closest friends, left the U.S. Postal squad. He wanted more money and independence, and decided he was tired of cycling on my behalf. So he defected. He accepted a larger contract offer, first from a team sponsored by the Linda McCartney food company. But that team proved short-lived and failed financially, so he accepted an offer from Deutsche Telekom, to work for my archrival, Jan Ullrich.

I couldn't believe it. Kevin and I had spent almost a decade cycling together. I'd ridden next to him, trained with him, climbed mountains with him. As a cyclist I felt I'd done a lot to help him, and as a friend I'd have killed for him, and I envisioned riding with him together to the ends of our careers. I felt totally betrayed: I was of the belief that when you had been friends for a decade, you didn't do what he did. "Colin Powell might as well have signed on to help the Chinese," I said.

Kevin and I stopped speaking, and the silence lasted for a while. Finally, we began to chat a little bit on the bike or when we ran into each other. Finally, through mutual friends acting as intermediaries, we sat down together and talked, finally cleared the air over an out-of-season bender. A couple of beers greased the skids to get two friends back together. The problem, perhaps, was that my expectations for Kevin weren't his own. It wasn't my right to determine what was best for his career.

But we have never cycled together again as teammates, and I still believe he never should have left. He ultimately fell out of love with the bike, and he quit the sport. (In fact, his retirement led to a kind of revenge on the drug testers. Early one morning in the fall of 2002, they showed up at his house, knocking on the door with their piece of paper. Kevin obliged them by peeing in a cup, and handed it over. "Here," he said. "I really hope you find something in it. I'm retired.")

We still hadn't hit the low point of the winter. That came when Kik and I failed in our attempt to have another child. In February, Kik underwent in-vitro fertilization, unsuccessfully.

It's hard to describe for the uninitiated how arduous the process was, the pills and self-administered shots and exams, with Kik cringing at the needles, only to hear that it hadn't worked. We'd assumed it would be as easy as when we had Luke. Nothing happened.

I took the call. Kik was looking right at me as I got the news, and she knew the answer was no. She could tell by my face and my tone. I said, as plainly as I could, "Okay, all right, thanks."

I hung up. "It's not the answer that we wanted," I said.

Kik teared up. "It's going to be okay," I said. But we were both crushed. "Well, look," I said. "We'll just try it again."

But trying again meant Kik would face constant needles, pills, sonograms. It meant she would have to stay home while I traveled, because she would have so many medical appointments. It meant longer separations, and all for another potential disappointment.

For a few days, we considered waiting another year. But that was doubly depressing, so we decided to start the cycle all over again.

The timing was hard: I was scheduled to go to an annual series of Postal training camps in preparation for the 2001 Tour, and in combination with Kik's IVF that meant more time apart from my family than ever. Luke was changing all the time, and I missed things.

He chattered away about "Da DEE this, and Da DEE that," and pointed to bicycles and said, "Da DEE?" And then finally, stated morosely, "Da DEE bye-bye."

I went to camp in Spain, and on my days off I looked for a new place to live. I finally found it, an ancient apartment in the town of Girona, a popular cycling haven. One of Kik's oldest friends, José Alvarez-Villar, lived 45 minutes away, and he helped with everything from finding a realtor to closing the deal with translators and attorneys.

I'd always loved Spain, and now I threw myself into renovating a lovely apartment that had been part of an old palace and needed special care. I set about finding artisans who could restore it—it gave me something to do other than simmer about the investigation.

We felt buffeted, between the separations, the investigation, the departure of my best friend to a rival's team, the decision to move, the difficulty of finding a new home, and a disappointing IVF treatment. But as lousy as those months were, Kik and I tried not to get too discouraged, because we always had illness as a context: career reversals and the indignities of a drug investigation couldn't scare us.

Whenever we needed a reminder of the difference between the small troubles we were experiencing and truly terrible vagaries, there was a cancer checkup.

I still visited my oncologist, Dr. Nichols, twice a year for blood work and scans, and it was always an uneasy experience. I wouldn't be declared formally cured until the five-year mark. That fall, Kik and I had flown to Oregon for my four-year exam.

The funny thing was, everyone thought I was done with cancer. They thought I'd beaten it, whipped it, willed it away. But surviving cancer was an evolution, rather than a limited experience confined to a time span or a location.

Some days the disease seemed like it had happened ages ago, and other days it seemed like it had happened yesterday. I had the odd sensation that I was still expelling poisons from my body, that there were still toxins in me. My body had been suffused not just with the scourging poisons of chemo, but also with anesthesia during two surgeries. Anesthesia could linger in the cells. It was a near-death experience; you were flooded with drugs, brought to a state of such deep, gassed unconsciousness that you were within a millimeter of death. And then they just held you there, chemically.

My head was shaved, and covered with small markers. The surgeon explained the procedure, as if he were talking about a piece of lumber.

"We're just going to cut a little hole, pop it out, remove the lesions, put it back in, and cover it up."

He was talking about my skull.

I still worried continually about my health. Little things other people might blow off, a bump, or an ache, provoked the thought, "My cancer is back." The slightest head cold was trouble around our house, and cause for in-depth analysis, deep pondering, and distress.

Even a little fatigue was a matter for concern and phone calls to my doctors and trainers. I was always putting socks on, never running around in bare feet, always with something on my neck. A sniffle was a case for long discussion, a bowl of hot soup, and a nap. If I didn't feel quite right or simply had a tired day on the bike, I was withdrawn, and you could feel the tension radiating off my body.

Kik and I arrived at the Oregon Health Sciences University in Portland for the battery of cancer tests. We always tried to treat the visit to Dr. Nichols like a routine checkup, but it wasn't. The results would be either perfect or terrible: I would be cancer-free or not. If the cancer came back, the only defense the second time around would be even more intense chemotherapy, and it wouldn't have very good odds of success.

I was tired when I woke up, tired when I ate, tired when I took a shower. I slept 20 hours a day; it was like taking the strongest sleeping pill known to man. One morning I was too tired to make it to the bathroom alone. "I think I'm going to be sick," I told my mother. She helped me out of the hospital bed and I leaned on her as I hobbled across the room, bent in half, my gown falling open.

I swore silently at the nurses who poked me with needles, drew blood, or took my blood pressure. I lay in bed, hemmed in by the colorless walls of the hospital room, a 10-by-14-foot rectangle with a window looking out on a brick building next door, with gray-green linoleum, beige walls, and light-brown blankets, but I was too tired to get up and do anything about it. Stapleton and Och and I played cards, games of hearts, until my eyes involuntarily closed again. We played so many card games we made up our own language. Jacks were Hooks, Kings were Cowboys. I stared balefully at the TV mounted in the corner. "I hate baseball," I said. I watched it anyway. I was too tired to change the channel.

The annual checkups always made Kik and me tense, but on this occasion we were especially so, given all that was going on in our lives. The doctors and nurses were far more confident about my health than I was, so perhaps they didn't realize how anxious we were.

A camera crew was on hand, doing an educational film about cancer, and they asked if they could film me as I went through the various cancer screenings. I agreed, but regretted it almost instantly.

I underwent a chest X ray, and thought, *Look, we don't know how this is going to come out. Get your camera out of here.*

As I went from scan to scan, there seemed to be people everywhere, nurses with a hundred things to sign, technicians who wanted to chat. Nobody seemed to realize that in a flashing moment on a CT scan screen we could see catastrophe. They were standing around, eating doughnuts, asking for autographs, taking pictures. To them, my good health was a foregone conclusion.

Suddenly, I wanted to be alone. I felt exposed. Rationally I knew the chances of the cancer coming back were negligible, but I still dreaded the test results. I'd do anything for the cancer community, show up anywhere, sign anything, or talk to anyone, but I didn't want to do it at that moment, because that moment still scared the crap out of me.

I just wanted to be a normal patient, to have some privacy and room for whatever might happen. Whether it was cause for relief, or something awful, I didn't want that moment captured.

The tests were fine.

"Everything looks good," Dr. Nichols said. Kik threw her arms around me, and I smiled with relief.

I never got accustomed to the attendant sensation: it was of sheer cleanliness. I was clean. My X rays and scans were the pictures of my well-being, literally the proof that my being was well. That sort of exposure I didn't mind. They showed the pictures of a man: five senses, an appetite, an admittedly selective intellect, an animal soul with a nervous system, four limbs and a backbone with vertebrae in various states of disrepair but not too bad, a pierce-mark on the chest, a horseshoe surgical dent in the scalp, a slash at the groin.

A little scarred-up in places and missing a thing or two, perhaps. But not much.

The investigative dossier the French accumulated on me got thicker. On the front cover of the folder was a picture of me, a Tour de France victory photo, as I rode down the Champs-Elysées with a flag.

On top of this, someone had superimposed a picture of a syringe. So much for the presumption of innocence, and the impartiality of the investigators.

The months passed, and still no test results came back. I was certain the samples were crystal clear—and surely they knew it too after all this time. It was hard to believe any amount of testing could take longer. But the prosecutors refused to confirm or to announce anything; instead they claimed they needed more tests and kept the case open.

Meanwhile, everyone who worked with me was guilty by association. My coach, Chris Carmichael, was raked by the press. Some journalists wrote that if I was on drugs he must have given them to me.

"Can you imagine?" Chris said. "You work your ass off, and then people say you didn't really do it."

I said, "Let it go. You're falling into their trap."

Chris was working with a hockey player named Saku Koivu, the captain of the Montréal Canadiens, who had been diagnosed with non-Hodgkins lymphoma and was attempting a remarkable comeback. Koivu was declared cancer-free just as the Canadiens were fighting for a playoff spot, and Chris was hired by George Gillett, the

Canadiens' owner, to help Koivu in his recovery. A month after Koivu finished chemo, Chris started him on a gradual daily regimen, with 30 minutes on a stationary bike and light weight-lifting. Soon Koivu was working out five hours a day, six days a week.

He came back before the end of the regular season, accounted for ten points in 12 games, and led the Canadiens to a victory in the playoffs as well. It was an unbelievable story.

"Was I doping him, too?" Chris asked, bitterly.

The investigation that should have concluded in January was still ongoing as spring approached. It was as though they had decided, "We'll keep testing until we find something." There was nothing I could do. I was used to controlling my own fate, whether on a bike or in business, or even in a sickbed, but now I was helpless.

Everything seemed to take forever, every minor legal point. The investigation would go quiet for long periods, and I wouldn't have any idea of what was going on, and it drove me crazy. I couldn't defend myself, couldn't talk to the judge or prosecutors, couldn't control the science, couldn't scream at anybody (except Bill), and I couldn't make it go faster. I hated all of these things, and in turn, I drove Bill crazy.

"What are we doing about it today?"

"Why is the judge always on vacation?"

"We're not doing enough. Why aren't we doing something?"

My lawyer in France wrote letters imploring the French authorities to speed up the investigation. I wrote the judge personally, offering my full cooperation. When the ICU balked at turning over my blood and urine to prosecutors in a jurisdictional quarrel, I asked the cycling authorities to please cooperate.

None of it made a difference. We had absolutely no influence over the speed at which the process moved, and that was hard for me. In fact, Bill came to believe that the more we tried to hurry them, the more likely they were to drag their feet. Sophie-Hélène Chateau had all the power and she could make it last as long as she wanted to.

At night I stared at the ceiling and thought about a worst-case scenario: what if the test results came back screwy because of bad science, or what if someone was so determined to find drugs that they rigged the results? If a false positive came back, all the world would ever remember about me was that I was a doper. The one verdict no one seemed willing to arrive at was that their case was baseless.

Bill tried to reassure me. "It'll be like this," he said. "All of a sudden we'll wake up one day, and it will be over, with just a little announcement that the investigation has come to a close."

"I don't know."

"You wait," he said. "This thing will go away in the dark of the night."

Finally, April came, and with it, what seemed to be good news. We heard via a reporter from Reuters that all of our tests were clean—exactly as we had insisted all along. My lawyer in Paris called the judge, Chateau. She confirmed it.

I was already in France for a bike race, and I went to Paris and called a press conference at the Hôtel George V to announce the results: all of the Postal team samples, not just mine, were negative. Nor had they found anything in our trash. Boxes and wrappers, that's all.

I couldn't help taking a few digs at the pace of the investigation, pointing out that while the press conference was going on, the judge was on vacation somewhere. "I'm losing sleep over this, I want my name exonerated, and she's on the beach for three weeks," I said. I added that I hoped the investigation would conclude swiftly now that there was positive proof that I was clean and so was our team.

But no sooner had I finished than Chateau began hedging. When reporters called her for confirmation, she admitted that our tests were negative—but she called my press conference "premature," and suggested that all of the evidence wasn't in.

A reporter mentioned that I hoped the investigation was drawing to a close.

She replied, curtly, "*Il rêve.*"

Translation: "He's dreaming."

Someone asked me what it would take to convince skeptics of my innocence. I answered, "I don't know." I was beginning to think I would be presumed guilty for the rest of my life.

Everything I had worked so hard for, my career, my reputation, what I'd done as an athlete, everything I had could go away, all the things you lose when people don't think you're a good guy.

What if I lost them? I had lost other things, and survived it. I thought about the things I could lose as a result of the doping charge, and wondered if I could do without them. My name was being attacked, and I felt that would be hard to replace. It was my own and no one else's, and it represented my values, my livelihood, and my family. I could do without money, or a Coca-Cola deal, but what if I lost my good name and my reputation? I might never be able to earn that back.

"It's so important to me," I told Kik. "Luke's name is Armstrong and people know that name, and when he goes to school I don't want them to say, 'Oh yeah, your dad's the big fake, the doper.' That would just kill me."

But there's one thing you can't lose, and that's yourself. I had my own innocence; that was something no one could mess with.

I'd lost races, health, and an old sense of self, and each loss had its own place in the scheme of a life. Other losses, if they came, would have their places, too. There are certain inevitabilities. You will grow older. You will be forced to compromise in ways you never imagined and confront problems you thought you were immune to. You will find a job, and perhaps lose it. You will fight with your mate, shoulder unwanted responsibilities, and cope with rank unfairness. You can allow all that to demoralize you. Or you can let it shape you, and trust that the shape will be more interesting because of it.

"Get altitude," Kik said.

That's what we tried to do. And then something happened that made it easier. In April, we found out that Kik was pregnant. In fact she was more than pregnant, she was *extremely* pregnant. She kept saying, "I feel so weird," and with good reason, as we were about to find out.

I was in Spain when she went to the obstetrician for an exam. She said to her doctor, Marco Uribe, "I'm scared that I'm having triplets."

He said, "Well, don't you want to know?"

She wasn't supposed to have a sonogram for another week and a half. But the doctor explained that if it was a multiple pregnancy perhaps he could see telltale signs.

"Do you want to see now?"

Kik was alone. It was about six o'clock at night, and half a world away, it was the middle of the night and I was sleeping. She hesitated, and then she said, "Yeah, I want to know. Of course I want to know."

He performed the sonogram, and there on the screen she saw it, a vibrant dual blip. Kik was going to wait until morning to call me, but she was so beside herself that she picked up her cell phone and dialed my number in Europe and left a message, her voice caught somewhere between profundity and weeping and hilarity, while I slept.

"It's twins," she said.

CHAPTER 4

Faith and Doubt

People give me things, things they want me to have, and things they suppose I need: bibles with my name inscribed, and prayer books, with passages marked. The main thing they seem to think I need is belief. I do believe, just not necessarily the same way they do. I'm a spiritual person who lacks a vocabulary for it. But that's asking for trouble.

A guy came up to me in an airport. "Lance, I want to talk to you about your relationship with God," he said.

"It's not going to be a long talk," I said.

Any account of my life begs for larger explanation: why did I live? I refuse the pat answer. God didn't do it. I don't mean to offend anyone, and I realize it upends the traditional expectation for me to say this, but I don't believe in a neat religious reckoning. I'm not much for prayer, don't belong to any religion that involves buildings, and I'm leery of proselytizing. Yet I wear a crucifix. How do I explain that to a stranger in an airport between flights?

What do I believe? I believe in mystery. I believe faith keeps a lot of the world straight. I believe if you squint hard and try to see the pattern of things, you can put them in their proper place: taxes, scandal, gossip, headache, traffic jams. I believe in restraint on the subject of religion, and I believe that the responsible person seriously questions it, because it's only right to question the administration of a church that shields child molesters, or the legitimacy of a faith that encourages repression and terror. Anything else is deficient use of your mind and morals.

I think too many people look to religion as an excuse, or a crutch, or a bailout. I think that what you've got is what you've got, here and now. Even when I was looking straight at death, I never thought there was something on the other end. J. Craig Ventner, in discussing the genome, said something that I'd never been able to articulate for myself, but which summed up everything I felt about cancer, and religion, and things in general.

"It's unequivocally clear that life begins at birth and ends at death," he said, "and if most people on this planet understood that, they would lead their lives very differently. We find religious or mysterious forces to fill in for our inadequacies, but heaven and hell are both here on earth every day, and we make our lives around them."

I viewed my cancer from a scientific standpoint. I was fighting a malignant cell that had invaded my body, and I wanted *scientific* tools with which to fight it, things I could measure: data, medicine, and information. I wanted to be as educated as possible about the illness, because statistics showed incontrovertibly that the more knowledgeable the cancer patient, the better his or her chances of survival. Studies also show that a person who has faith has a higher-quality experience. I don't deny that. All I mean to say is that when I was sick I saw too many people who evaded personal responsibility, wouldn't take a role in the cure. I flinched each time I heard someone say, "It's in God's hands," or, "God will provide."

I was sleeping so much that I wondered if sleeping was almost like dying. Maybe I was dying. "Am I?" I wondered. You believe you'll live, but you don't know.

My friend Scott MacEachern from Nike came to visit me. He knocked on the front door and I answered, standing in the foyer of my big house, all by myself, with no hair, no eyebrows, and my face drawn. It was the first time Scott had seen me since I'd gotten sick. While we were still standing there, I dipped my head and showed Scott the big horseshoe scars from my brain surgery, and then I lifted up my shirt and showed him the other places where they had cut me.

That evening Scott and I sat around and talked about the illness, and about life after death. I remember the flow of our conversation, and being scared but trying to be courageous, and telling him that I was trying to stay in front of it and to educate myself, and that I was so tired, but that I was determined, too.

The next morning Scott got up and went for a run, and when he came back, he heard music blasting from the garage. Scott walked around the house and peered into the garage. I was inside, astride a stationary bike. I was clipped into the trainer, in my cycling shoes and shorts, bald as a cue ball and cut up.

I was out of the saddle. I was attacking, on the trainer. Scott told me later, "I knew at that point that whether you lived or died, either way, there was a fight going on."

None of these tendencies of mine meets with the usual definition of spirituality. Some people even see me as a cause, "There's a guy that needs help."

But I can live with the conflict, if you want to call it "conflict." I'm conflicted for a good reason: when I was a boy I got a poor impression of organized religion. My stepfather, Terry Armstrong, was a church deacon—but that didn't prevent him from mistreating my mother or beating me with a paddle. So I saw religion as something to distrust, that could be used as an instrument of fear as well as good, and just because people went to church every Sunday didn't mean they weren't corrupt.

My children are being reared as Catholics, and their mother is a practicing Catholic. My own house is open on the subject. I never argued with Kik about what the kids should be taught, or how they should be raised; as far as I was concerned they should go to church with their mother. I think that by and by, the kids will be smart enough, and, I hope, independent enough, to make their own decisions, and if they are believers, all the better.

Kik is increasingly passionate about her faith, while I've remained a skeptic. We were married in a Catholic church, but over the years it became an issue of divergence. My doubt could occasionally upset her. Sometimes a stranger would stop us, and say to me, "Why don't you pray?" Kik would say, "If it makes you feel any better, I pray for him."

Also, I had a tendency to be a smart-aleck that didn't sit well with her.

When she'd go to mass, I'd make a comment.

"What are you doing that for?"

"I like going to mass."

"But it's Saturday. Let's go to dinner instead."

"I like Saturday mass."

I'd think about that for a second.

"Can't you change it?" I'd crack.

But one day she cured me, convinced me it wasn't worth making any more cracks. "Wherever my strength comes from, you should be happy for it," she said. "Because you rely on me a lot, so you rely on that strength." She had a point; if faith affected her life, then by extension if affected mine. When I raced, Kik would find a church and light candles for me, and I appreciated it. During the Tour I'd ask her, "Did you light a candle for me today?" But nobody in the family ever said, "You want to go to church with us?" They knew better.

Kik started talking to Luke early on about Jesus Christ, but Christmas wasn't especially meaningful to me, except as it related to my children. On the morning of Luke's second Christmas, I was beside myself with excitement, and I was the first to wake up. We'd gotten him a little battery-operated jeep, and I couldn't wait to see his face when he opened the box. But on that morning, of all mornings, he decided to sleep in. I paced the kitchen impatiently. Kik and her parents, Dave and Ethel Richard, got up, and we all sat in the kitchen drinking coffee and reading the paper. Finally I couldn't stand it anymore.

"Let's just go get him up," I said.

I got out of my chair and grabbed a Christmas stocking with bells on it, and I went upstairs, and I stood outside Luke's room and I shook it, hard. Nothing. So I shook it again, and again, impatiently. Downstairs Kik collapsed in giggles because she could hear the Christmas bells, and me shouting, "Ho! Ho! Ho!" Finally, my son poked his head out of bed.

Kik thought my skepticism was based on childhood resentment and that eventually I might be persuadable on the subject, might some day "credit the source" of my survival. I disagreed, and still do. But it doesn't prevent me from being respectful of and even intrigued by some aspects of faith, particularly by the ceremony and imagery of it.

It's why I wear the cross on my chest—it's an expression of kinship with those who've suffered. While I was still in remission, my friend Stacy Pounds, who worked for Bill Stapleton as an assistant for many years, was diagnosed with lung cancer. My mother bought a pair of silver crucifixes, and Stacy wore one, and I wore the other. I still wear it.

In the winter and spring of 2001, in the midst of preparing for another Tour de France, I became absorbed in restoring the old family chapel in our new home in Girona. I'd bought the first floor of what had once been a small palace on one of the most historic streets in the old city, in part because I was stunned by the wrecked beauty of it, and also because I knew how it would please Kik. The apartment was dank and crumbling, would have to be completely redesigned and restored, but you couldn't help but feel remnants in the air of all that had happened there, the fervency in the flaked and fading walls, the aged dank gray stone, the arched gothic ceilings, and the colored glass.

Girona is a living archaeological dig, with the ruins from different ages, elements of Roman, Moorish, Jewish, Muslim, and medieval history, still visible. The gothic cathedral is one of the largest in Europe, and it's just up a winding, narrow cobbled street, lined with small bookshops, cafés, and other businesses. According to the history books, during some of the bloodier periods in the city's intensely religious history, rivulets of blood literally ran down the street to the bottom of the hill.

The apartment has tall windows with a wrought-iron terrace, and I can step outside and look down on my favorite sidewalk café directly across the street, where there are deep wicker chairs in which you can settle and drink coffee. The apartment itself has the old

gothic arches and cornices, and two small gardens, with stone fountains gurgling. But the centerpiece is the small family chapel, with
deep blue walls and gilt stars and a small wooden altar.

I hired craftswomen from Barcelona to repair the frescoed walls,
matching the midnight-blue and magenta walls with textured gilt details, and when it was done, I bought a painting for it, an exquisite
piece of 15th-century religious art, to be the centerpiece over the
altar.

To me, that chapel isn't just about worship, but about history,
about age, about the hundreds of years that have seeped into the
arched ceilings, the gold paint, and the original stained glass. It's
stunning. I appreciate that chapel as a balance to logic; some things
can be measured, and other things can't.

My survival is an immeasurable thing, too. How much of it was
due to science, how much to belief, how much to self-will? I don't
know the answer, and I resist the simple, comfortable explanations,
because frankly, pure luck had a good deal to do with it, too. Sometimes *I don't know* is the best and most honest answer you can give.

In 2001, as I approached the five-year cancer anniversary and
the prospect that I'd be declared officially cured, I had reason to consider all of these issues again. I also had yet another reason to try to
win the Tour again. The race was always a reconfirmation, another
act of continued existence. It seemed only right to exhaust the possibility in the body I'd been given back. Regardless of what you at-
tributed my ongoing presence to, it seemed to me that I was obliged
to *do* something with it.

And racing is what I do. But it was beginning to occur to me that
it's also the *easiest* thing I do. It was a lot easier than, say, defending

myself from a drug investigation, holding together a marriage, or trying to reconcile the conflict between faith and science.

Early that spring I visited Lourdes, not to light candles or bathe in the waters, but to ride my bike in the mountains above the city.

One day, I ascended seven mountain passes over a distance of 130 miles. Some of the peaks were snowed in and I couldn't get to them. I'd go as far as I could, turn my bike around and coast to the bottom, and then ride up again, just to get another big climb in.

Obsessive training was one way to escape the frustrations of the drug inquiry, which still dragged on. First the French authorities said it would conclude before the Tour, but it remained open. The assistant prosecutor, François Franchi, had asked for a new round of tests—for what, he couldn't say. "For now we haven't found any EPO," he said. "We don't have anything concrete or positive." They continued to try in vain to find something in my urine.

My friend Robin Williams joked, "What is it, a chardonnay? It gets better with age?"

The best revenge, I decided, was to win the Tour again. Another victory might not satisfy the skeptics, but at least it would satisfy me.

This time, my son would be old enough to understand a little bit of what I did for a living. I schooled him well.

"Who's going to win?" I'd ask him.

"DADDY!" he'd yell.

The Tour began on the coast of northern France, at Dunkirk, with a short prologue in the rain to a seafront finish. Luke loved being at the race. He hung out with me at the team bus and showed off all the words he knew, by pointing to a bike, wheel, truck, and so on. He kept offering me bites of his sandwich as I warmed up for the prologue. I politely declined—it wasn't the ideal pre-race snack.

"What is Daddy's color?" I asked.

"Yo-yo," he answered.

He couldn't really say yellow, so everything was yo-yo, all day long. Yo-yo bus, yo-yo bike, yo-yo truck . . . you get the idea. It was a constant yo-yo commentary.

I grinned at the start—I'd been waiting for this moment. I beat the pedals down the straightaway, and across the rain-slick streets of Dunkirk. But I finished a faintly disappointing third. Daddy wasn't wearing yo-yo. Luke would have to wait—for longer than anyone expected.

We wound through northeastern France, racing parallel to the English Channel, and Jan Ullrich and I marked each other. Once again, he was the rider to beat, the most talented and credible challenger in the peloton. He came into the race superbly fit, in much better form than in the previous year, with jutting cheekbones and muscles bulging under his racing skins. "It's now or never," Ullrich declared.

We went to Verdun, the garrison town about 160 miles from Paris where 600,000 soldiers from France and Germany and America lost their lives in World War I, and where I'd won my first Tour stage in 1993. This time, we raced in a team time trial. The 41.5-mile course was buffeted by wind and rain, and about halfway through, two of our Postal riders, Christian Vande Velde and Roberto Heras, hit a newly painted road line. Vande Velde's bike skidded out from under him, and their wheels touched. They went down in a clattering heap. Roberto would ride sorely for a week. Incredibly, two days later Christian crashed into a lamppost and had to abandon the Tour.

We rode on for days through a relentless downpour. Finally, we turned away from the coast and toward the mountains, and after eight stages we reached the foothills of the Alps.

By the time we arrived, we were behind, badly. A previously unsung French rider named François Simon and a talented young Kazakh named Andreï Kivilev had succeeded in a major breakaway, and Simon was the leader in the yellow jersey—by a huge margin of 35 minutes. It had happened because we were too conservative. When they got down the road, nobody wanted to chase them down—we thought it was more important to conserve our strength as much as possible early in the race, and so did everybody else. It was like a poker game to see who was bluffing, only nobody was willing to put their cards on the table, so Simon opened his huge gap unchallenged. I was well back in 24th place, and Ullrich was in 27th.

There would be some long, hard days of chasing ahead, particularly given the presence of Kivilev. Simon was not a climber and we all knew he would recede in the mountains. But Kivilev, a 27-year-old riding for Cofidis, was in fourth place, 13:12 ahead of me, and I suspected he wouldn't go away. I'd been watching him for some time, and what I saw was a cyclist who was rising fast to the top of the sport, who had both work ethic and ability. The truth was, I wished he was on my team instead of someone else's. But what I couldn't know at the time was that Andreï would never get the chance to fulfill his potential: two years later, he would be killed in a high-speed crash. His performance in this Tour would become a haunting suggestion of what might have been.

The breakaway blew up Johan's carefully plotted race plan for our Postal team. We had to sit down and make a new strategy. Johan kept calm. We would simply have to ride harder, he said; it would

take us a few days longer to get the yellow jersey. "We'll have to attack at every opportunity," he said.

Once again the first mountain stage would be critical, psychologically and physically. The mountains were always where the field
sorted itself out, and where real fitness prevailed. In this Tour, the
first mountain stage would be the Alpe d'Huez, which was among
the most mythically cruel mountains in France.

It was a stage of 130 miles, with 6,000 feet of climbing over
three big peaks rated *hors de catégorie*—beyond category in difficulty.
But the first two climbs were mere precursors to the Alpe d'Huez, a
steep 12 miles up with 21 switchbacks.

I wanted the Alpe d'Huez. It's among the most famous and most
historically revered climbs in the Tour de France. It's not very long,
but it's very steep, and all of the switchbacks have been numbered,
and on every number a former winner's name is written. It's a cycling
lover's climb.

But as a team, we were not in good shape. It had been a hard first
week, between the rain and a constant crosswind on the roads. Christian was out. Roberto had tendinitis in his knee, which was heavily
bandaged. Also, Tyler Hamilton had crashed on a stage to Antwerp,
and had tendinitis all through his left arm and wrist. Those of us who
weren't outright injured were sore and tired. The wind meant you
could never take a rest on the bike, and the cost was beginning to
show. The effects of the Tour were cumulative; every day took a little
more away from your legs.

With so many riders on our team injured or not feeling well, we
had doubts about how we would hold up over those three peaks. I
was feeling okay—but I couldn't ride at the front all by myself and
still expect to have anything left for the Alpe d'Huez.

Meanwhile, Ullrich's Deutsche Telekom team looked strong and healthy to a man—and leading Ullrich up the mountains would be my old friend Kevin Livingston.

That morning, Ullrich and his team did the hard work early, riding at the front of the peloton. We hung back and paced ourselves. Sometimes you have to be flexible; to employ a different style of riding than you're accustomed to.

I radioed Johan that I wanted to come back to the car. Johan sped up, and I drifted over to talk to him. As I rode parallel to the car window, we discussed the situation. "Maybe it's not a bad thing to show some weakness," Johan said. "If they think you're in bad shape, they'll ride harder. We'll relax until the bottom of the Alpe d'Huez. And then we go."

Basically, Johan wanted me to bluff. By feigning fatigue, I might sucker Telecom into spending too much energy trying to put me away. I'd have to be both an actor and a cyclist for much of the day. But if it worked, it would give us a better chance of winning the stage, we decided.

As we rode up the first severe peak, the Col de Madeleine, I sagged over my handlebars and grimaced. The first mountain stage is always a shock to the body, and the riders who aren't in great shape can crack right away. Halfway up the Madeleine, three riders abandoned the race—pulled over and quit. I acted as though I might soon join them. I lagged at the back of the peloton, in the posture of a suffering dog, head hanging, as if I'd rather be anywhere but on a bike. Other riders began to wonder if I was sick, and so did the television announcers covering the race. Even my own teammates were a little anxious.

Each team had a follow car with a TV in it, from which the race directors watched the action carefully and listened to the comments from other teams. Later, it would be hugely entertaining to watch a replay of the race and listen to the announcers. My friend, commentator Paul Sherwen, called the action for the U.S. telecast. "Armstrong looking in a spot of trouble," he said.

I slogged along at the back of the group. The back was where the hangers-on were, barely keeping pace. A rider at the back was a rider in for a long day. "We haven't seen Lance Armstrong riding anywhere near the front of this group," Sherwen said. "He's having a rough ride."

Ullrich and his Telekom teammates took the bait—they surged to the front and started riding at a hot tempo, excited. Clearly, they had gotten the message that I was hurting. They responded exactly as Johan had predicted they would. They did all the work at the front, while we drafted at the back.

For the next several hours, Telekom led the peloton. They pumped at their pedals up and down the mountain passes, for miles and miles. Meantime, I rode along looking weak. I sucked water from a bottle, I hung my head, and my chest heaved with the supreme effort of turning the wheels.

My teammate José Luis "Chechu" Rubiera faded back to the car to pick up more water bottles, as if I needed them. Johan handed several bottles through the window to Rubiera. "There's obviously a problem here for Armstrong," Sherwen reported. ". . . Armstrong is obviously drinking an awful lot of liquid today."

Johan asked Chechu how I was really doing. "Hey, he is flying," Chechu said. "He's just easy."

A member of the TV press came by on a motorbike and interviewed Johan through the window of his car. Johan knew that whatever he said would be picked up by the other teams, listening to the coverage.

"I don't know what's happening," Johan said. "This is not normal for Lance, I've never seen him like that, and the rest of the team is not so good, either. So for the moment we'll just try to survive."

At the front, Telekom drove on all the harder, surging. The road began to bite into everyone's legs. The hillsides were verdant and grew steeper. The road narrowed, and the cliffs crept closer to our shoulders, and around corners you could see glaciers in the distance.

The announcers continued to provide useful commentary on my weak form. "It's a long way back to see Armstrong, he does not look good, and he should not be riding so far down the group, he's obviously having a horrendous day."

We went over the top of another big climb, the Col du Glandon, and headed down the most beautiful descent in the entire Tour, past a dammed lake at the bottom of an undulating, green valley, with jagged ice peaks looming.

"Don't you think we should move to the front?" Chechu asked.

"Just wait," I said. I added, in Spanish, "*Miramos, esperamos, decidimos, atacamos.*"

"Let's see, let's wait, let's decide, and then attack."

I slipped up to 12th place over the Glandon. We skirted a lake, and ran along the edge of a giant granite cliff. The shifting temperatures began to get to us; it was hot in the valleys and cold on the peaks, and the disparity made your muscles seize up.

The stage leader up to that point was a Frenchman, Laurent Roux. Ullrich and I were more than seven minutes behind.

"Just a little?" Chechu asked. "Shouldn't you move up just a little?"

"Chechu," I said. "*Miramos, esperamos, decidimos, atacamos.*"

Johan drove the team car up, and I consulted with him in person. Johan stuck his head out the window and I rode close to the car. Over the years, I've picked up some Flemish from Johan, and as we put our heads together, we talked half in English and half in Flemish.

"Okay, this looks great," he said. "Everything's perfect. When we get to the bottom of the Alpe d'Huez, that's when you go. And when you go, go *vollebak.*"

Vollebak means "full gas." Floor it.

"*Vollebak*," he said again. "You got it?"

"You're going to see *vollebak* like you've never seen *vollebak*," I said.

I rejoined Chechu. We began to approach the Alpe d'Huez. Ullrich was still riding at the front.

Chechu said, "Now?"

"Okay. Watch the show," I said.

We surged forward. The huge crowds on the sides of the road seemed to part as we accelerated.

We swooped over a bridge, passed a rushing white waterfall. We came around a long, sweeping left-hand turn—and hit the foot of the mountain. The road kicked up.

There was Ullrich just ahead.

I raced up to his wheel.

"Armstrong has maybe been playing an incredible poker game

today by sitting at the back and letting everybody else do the work," Sherwen said.

I locked onto the back of Ullrich's bike, with Chechu next to me.

Until that moment, Ullrich had thought I was done. All he had heard all day was that I was hurting and out of contention. And now here I was.

I passed him.

I purposefully looked over my shoulder. I stared into Ullrich's sunglasses for a long moment.

It was important to really look at the face of a rival: a guy's mouth, the way he's sweating, and whether he's squinting behind his glasses. The look told you everything: whether he was tired or fresh, how much he had left in him. Ullrich was clearly hurting. His earpiece dangled down, his jersey hung open, and so did his mouth.

I stared over my shoulder for a moment longer, and later spectators would say it seemed I was taunting Ullrich, as if I was saying, "I've been playing with you all day, and now the real race is just starting. Catch me if you can." But the truth is that I was checking to see what the shape of the other riders was, too. I wasn't looking only at Ullrich—I was looking over his shoulder. What I saw convinced me to make my move.

I faced front again. I stood up on the pedals, and took off.

I was gone. Within seconds I was out of his view. It was a shock tactic, totally spontaneous, and it worked. With that one acceleration, I was away, and Ullrich couldn't respond.

Johan babbled excitedly in my ear. "He's dropped, he's dropped!"

I steadily lengthened the lead, ticking my legs over. As I worked uphill, here came the last man between me and the finish line, Laurent Roux, who had started the climb with a seven-minute lead. I passed him.

I kept my eyes trained on the road just ahead of me, sightless except for the next hairpin turn. About halfway up the climb, I thought I passed Chris Carmichael standing on the mountainside, grinning like an idiot. I noted that he was wearing a pair of electric-blue Oakley shoes.

I crossed the finish line. I bared my teeth and shook my fists so hard I nearly threw myself off the bike. I had been riding for six hours and 23 minutes.

I braked and dropped off the bike, exhausted. We'd won one of the most famous of Tour stages, on a day when no one expected me to, and with tactics rather than aggression. It was as oddly satisfying as any stage victory could be. We'd never be able to use the same trick again—but it had succeeded this once.

Later, Carmichael came to visit me at the team hotel. I said, "You were wearing those ugly-ass shoes, weren't you? I saw those shoes. Carmichael, how can you wear those things?"

I wanted that yellow jersey. I wanted to pull it on and show it to my son, so he could say, "Yo-yo, Daddy." But I was still riding from behind; despite the Alpe d'Huez performance, I continued to trail the overall leader, Simon.

Luke and Kik arrived the next day, in time to see me win a romantic time-trial stage in the mountains, from the ski town of Grenoble to the winter resort of Chamrousse. It moved me into third place overall, still chasing Simon. But something far more significant happened that day.

Kik met me at the finish line, and we went to our hotel, so we could have a few minutes to ourselves in my room before dinner. She pulled out an envelope. In it was the result of the ultrasound test that would tell us whether the babies she was carrying were boys or girls.

When we had decided to try in-vitro a second time that fall, we knew it meant that Kik would have to go through part of the process alone, because of my training schedule. Before, we had carefully planned our attempts to get pregnant in the off-season so that I could be with her for her appointments, but this time we didn't have that choice; if we wanted another baby, Kik would have to do it while I was racing. She had found out we were having twins without me. We didn't want her to find anything else out by herself, or have any more long-distance phone conversations.

Instead, she asked the doctor to write the answer down on a piece of paper and seal it in an envelope. Kik carried the envelope home and sat it on a desk for several days, and then packed it in her backpack.

It was a beautiful alpine evening as Kik and I lounged in my hotel room, which looked out on the village. From the window we could see her parents down below, having a drink and relaxing at a sidewalk café table, along with Bill Stapleton and Bart Knaggs, while Luke ran around on a grassy lawn.

Kik took the envelope out of her backpack, and announced that she was so nervous she had sweaty palms.

"Give me that," I said.

I snatched it out of her hand, while Kik giggled. I tore it open, stared at the sheet of paper, and threw back my head and shouted with laughter.

"Let me see, let me see," Kik said.

I teased her for a moment, holding the paper above my head, and then I gave it to her. Kik glanced down and saw the number 2, and the letter "g." For an instant she misread it, she thought it said, "*garçons,*" French for "boys," but then she looked again and it said, "Two girls, congratulations." Kik squealed in delight.

For some reason it was the last thing we expected. I'd loved the idea of twins from the get-go; I was fascinated by the possibility, the uniqueness and yet sameness of them. We talked about two boys, or a boy and a girl, but the notion of twin girls simply never occurred to us. Now that they were a reality, we were ecstatic. Bart Knaggs and his wife, Barbara, had twin girls. They were beaming comical little blond things, and Bart had taught them each to say, "I'm a genius!" Now that we'd have our own set, it seemed to me a beautiful completion of our family chemistry, to have a pair of female counterparts to Luke.

I hugged Kik and stuck my head into the hallway and yelled the news to my teammates. Then I went over to the window and threw it open, and leaned out over that beautiful span of grass, and I shouted the news out the window.

"Hey, Ethel!" I yelled down to Kik's mother.

"Yeah!" she answered, looking up.

"It's two girls!" I yelled.

The whole terrace erupted. Everyone below screamed and cheered. Ethel wept, and then Kik wept and we just stood there waving the piece of paper out the window. A little later, we came down and had dinner with everybody, and toasted our daughters.

The family visit was only a brief respite from racing. Over the next couple of days, we rode deep into the Pyrenees. It was a different kind of scenery; the Alps were covered with industrial towns or ski resorts with condo developments big as skyscrapers, but the Pyrenees were wilder, smaller yet somehow more dramatic, with long green valleys and snow-capped peaks. As we rode, the mountains kept taking their toll. Another rider, Christophe Moreau of France, threw his bike down in disgust and quit the race with lung problems.

Ullrich and I continued to shadow each other, sometimes riding side by side. He crunched his large gears while I bobbed up and down on the pedals in smaller gears. The difference in our styles was visible: he pedaled 75 times a minute, while I pedaled 90. He was a big, rolling, pantherish rider, while I looked, someone said, like a cat climbing a tree.

Simon was still 13 minutes ahead of both of us, in first place. But in the Pyrenees we faced three huge mountain stages, with a total of 11 major peaks to climb. We knew the day would come when Simon would break, and suspected it would come on a grueling climbing stage called Pla d'Adet, a long, 120-mile day that would take us over six peaks.

The stage took us past the place where my old friend Fabio Casartelli had died during a Tour descent in 1995. A beautiful marble monument marked the place, and during the spring in training I'd pulled over and stood in the mist. The other Postal riders went on, but I stayed for a few long minutes. I was taken aback by how much emotion I still felt each time I rode past, and I remembered how I'd sobbed in my hotel room.

But during the race itself I didn't have time to contemplate. There was too much else to pay attention to, between Ullrich, Simon, the pursuit of the yellow jersey, and the constant climbing and descending.

Shortly before we reached the final climb, something frightening happened that reminded us all again of just how perilous and tragic the sport could be. I was riding just behind Ullrich on a difficult descent at about 50 miles per hour. There weren't many turns, but it was fast, and there was gravel that made your wheels slide around.

Ullrich glanced back over his shoulder for his teammates, and fussed with his microphone. He reached for his mike with one hand, and began talking into it. He pulled the mike closer and ducked his head; it was hard to communicate in the wind from the speeding descent.

Ahead, a turn came up.

He didn't see it.

I thought, *Uh-oh.* I was already leaning on my own brakes. *He'd better brake,* I thought. *Why doesn't he brake?*

Ullrich's head came up, but not in time. He sailed straight over the shoulder of the road and down a precipice. One second he was there and the next he had vanished.

It looked horrific—like he had gone headfirst over a cliff.

He's finished, I thought. I immediately slowed down and radioed Johan to see if Ullrich was all right.

As I slowed down, other riders did, too. Kevin Livingston pulled over, and stopped. "We're waiting," I told the other riders. "We're all going to wait for him."

After a moment, Johan radioed me to say that he could see Ullrich climbing up the cliffside, and he seemed fine. Luckily, he had fallen onto a grassy bank of a steep gully, and was struggling to get his bike upright and rejoin the race.

I continued to ride slowly, waiting for Ullrich to catch up. This was what racing custom dictated. It's not something American audiences necessarily understand, but it's an intrinsic part of the sport and any other top rider would have done the same for a respected opponent.

Ullrich deserved the respect of the entire peloton. He had never broken; he fell back, but he always fought to the head of the pack again, and I could never completely ride away from him. No matter what, he was always there, next to my shoulder, unwilling to concede the race. You should always honor your fiercest opponent: the better your opponent, the better you have to be.

He caught up to me. I said, "You okay?" He nodded. "I'm fine," he said. We accelerated up the road. We resumed race pace, and stayed shoulder to shoulder, dead-even until the last 3.7 miles.

The final climb, to Pla d'Adet, was one that I knew well: I'd rehearsed it three different times in the spring, studying the steep parts. It was a slope where you could put some time between yourself and the other riders, and now I was ready to. Much as I admired Ullrich and was glad he was all right, I wanted to get rid of him now. I wanted that yellow jersey, and a stage win would give it to me. I thought, *Yo-yo Daddy*.

When we hit the final climb, I jumped out of my seat and charged. Ullrich made no real attempt to follow. Within seconds it seemed like I was 100 yards ahead of him. Behind me, he put his head down and kept on.

I rode on alone, and within a half-mile I passed the last cyclist ahead of me, Laurent Jalabert of France. Later Jalabert said, "He made it look so easy that it was beautiful."

But Jalabert was wrong, it wasn't easy. It hurt, deep inside where muscle met bone. I simply pretended it didn't hurt, controlling my demeanor. I understood how demoralizing it was to spend a day like that on a bike and get passed by a rider who doesn't seem to suffer. It's a mental and physical defeatedness that no one else knows except the cyclists themselves.

Of course it hurt. If you looked closely you could see that it did, in my bloodshot eyes. The truth is that there's no such thing as riding effortlessly in the Tour. It simply didn't hurt as much as it could have, because all the training I had done through the year paid dividends. I was well prepared, I knew which parts of the mountain were the worst, and I'd learned to use even, consistent efforts, and avoid crises. But it still hurt.

I crossed the finish line alone, and toppled off the bike, spent, the new leader of the Tour de France. We had done what Johan asked, and attacked at every opportunity—and the result was that we had won three of the last four stages, and made up 35 minutes and 24 places in the standings. In two days alone, we'd made up 22 minutes. It was the second–biggest deficit ever overcome.

Johan pulled up in the team car, exultant. That day, he had a passenger, Phil Knight, the co-founder of Nike. Knight had been to virtually every great event in the world, and witnessed countless thrilling moments, but he had never seen a Tour de France stage before, and now as he climbed from the car, he looked stunned by it all: the rainbow colors of the peloton jet-streaming by, the wrecks and recoveries, the precipitous climbs under scorching sun. I looked at his face and knew we'd created another cycling enthusiast. "That is the single greatest day in sport that I have ever seen," Knight raved.

At last I pulled the yellow jersey over my shoulders. It was a relief to wear that garment I'd been chasing so hard.

Ullrich and I continued our epic battle through the rest of the Pyrenees, sweat pouring off our chins in the high heat of the mountains. On the last of the mountain stages, after we had mounted the massive 6,938-foot Col du Tourmalet, Ullrich slipped ahead of me across the finish line, to win the stage. As he did so, he dropped a hand and trailed it behind him, reaching out for mine. I grasped it.

I didn't know exactly what he meant by it, but I guessed it had something to do with companionship. We had ridden hard together. He may have meant it as a kind of congratulations, too, because afterward, he conceded the race. I had a five-minute lead, which now seemed safe—all I had to do was stay upright until we reached Paris.

"I'm finished," Jan said. "I had no chance this year against Lance. I'm not sure I did anything wrong. I left the other guys behind me."

The victory was assured, but there was one last thing to do before I stepped onto the winner's podium: address the doping suspicions. The topic had dogged me for months, and it had never waned throughout the race. A headline in *L'Equipe* said, MUST WE BELIEVE IN ARMSTRONG? The article said, "There are too many rumors, too many suspicions. He inspires both admiration and rejection." Along the course, some French spectators had booed me.

It was traditional for the wearer of the yellow jersey to hold a press conference before arriving in Paris, and I was looking forward to it. I wanted to face the skeptics and the accusers and look them in the eye. I wanted to answer the charges, and I wanted to declare my innocence.

About 300 reporters showed up, and for over an hour, I fielded every inquiry they could fire at me.

"I've lived by the rules," I said. I pointed out that I'd been tested no fewer than 30 times in the past Tours, and never once had I failed. "The proof is there," I said to one reporter. "You just don't want to believe that."

I added that I would never take a substance like EPO or human growth hormone and jeopardize my health after what I'd been through.

"I give everything I've got," I said. My performances were the result of hard work; of the fact that I had trained and been on the bike when no one else was riding, in the off-season and in all weather. I'd ridden the Alps in the snow. "And I didn't see any other riders there," I said.

The innocent, I said, could never prove their innocence. How could you prove a negative?

Another reporter rose and questioned me about an Italian doctor named Michele Ferrari, who had come under investigation for doping. He had also made an unfortunate and ill-considered remark back in 1994, when he said that EPO was "no more harmful than orange juice." His files had been seized, and in them was a reference to me. Now my association with him was, to some people, further evidence that I was a doper.

I knew Michele Ferrari well; he was a friend and I went to him for occasional advice on training, I said. He wasn't one of my major advisors, but he was one of the best minds in cycling, and sometimes I consulted him. He had instructed me in altitude training and advised me about my diet. (The fact was that Ferrari, no matter what else you thought of him, was an expert analyst. He understood the combination of technique and physiology as few people did, and he could discuss everything from chainrings to wattages with authority. He had a precision of knowledge that I appreciated.)

I refused to turn on Michele, or to apologize for knowing him, and as far as I could tell, there was no evidence against him. The investigation was based on the fact that, a few years earlier, he had treated a cyclist named Filippo Simeoni, who was later found to have doped. "He's innocent until a trial proves otherwise," I said.

The reporter asked me how I could square an anti-drug stance with maintaining a relationship with Ferrari. "It's my choice," I said. "I believe he's an honest man, a fair man, and an innocent man. Let there be a trial. With what I've seen with my own two eyes and my experience, how can I prosecute a man whom I've never seen do anything guilty?"

I said that I knew the legitimacy of the entire sport of cycling was in question, and that I'd become the lightning rod for it. "Cycling is under the microscope and I have to answer for that, and I'm fine with it," I said. But I found it sad that the Tour had become an event so permeated by suspicion.

"It's a race; it shouldn't become a trial," I said.

Finally, I rose. I said all I had left to say: "I leave here an honest man, a happy man, and hopefully a winner." And I left the room.

"I needed that," I said to Bill on the way out.

There were no more challenges the rest of the way to Paris, on or off the bike. We simply rode and enjoyed the view, of those fields and fields and fields of sunflowers.

By the time we crossed the finish line on the Champs-Elysées, we'd ridden 2,150 miles—in 86 hours, 17 minutes, and 28 seconds, to be precise. I took deep satisfaction in the performance, because it had been a race won with tactics as well as strength, and Postal had become a more complete and mature team.

Ullrich's team leader, Rudy Pevenage, paid us a funny compliment. "We keep waiting for Armstrong to have a bad day," he said. "But the only bad day he has is the morning-after hangover in Paris."

There was something straightforward about the formula of training and racing: I worked hard and I won. A race was a simple undertaking, with a start and a finish line, and the outcome determined by skill. You either won or lost, and the concreteness of that answer was comforting. What else could you say that about?

Nothing—especially not after September 11.

I flew back to the States and stopped in New York for a couple of days. I disappeared for an afternoon, and no one could find me. Finally, I came back to the hotel.

I'd been riding my bike in Central Park.

I loved New York; it was a grand phosphorescent city, and it had been good to me personally. By now I knew it pretty well because I had to pass through all the time on my way to Europe. Walking or biking around town was like negotiating an obstacle course, and it gave me a sense of accomplishment. Once you learned to love New York, you loved it more, and more complicatedly, than other places.

It's said that September 11 happened to everyone, and it did. But it happened to New Yorkers, first, and foremost, and worst.

That morning, I was at home in Austin, just another father watching *Sesame Street* with my small son. The phone rang, and I picked it up and Bill Stapleton said, "You better turn on the news." I flipped over to a cable news channel, and I couldn't believe my eyes. I sat there, helpless, staring at the horrible displacement of the skyline.

Shortly after September 11, the Red Cross called, wondering if I would come to New York and help boost the morale of the firefighters and rescue workers, as a way to thank them. I accepted immediately—I wasn't sure a goodwill visit from me meant much, but I hated just sitting and watching at home in Texas, and it would give me a chance to do something. I said I would like to go unannounced, with one rule: no press.

I asked Bart Knaggs to come with me, and together we flew to New York on the evening of September 20. All the major airports were still closed, so we landed at a private airport in White Plains. I remember that as we flew over the city, AC/DC's "Back in Black" was playing on the plane's sound system, and it seemed appropriately dark. A friend from Nike, Dave Mingey, met us when we landed, along with representatives from the Red Cross; they had worked together to set up my tour of the city.

We went straight to a pier on the Hudson River that had been transformed into a makeshift command center. It resembled the active floor of a business convention, with hundreds of people, from the fire department to the Coast Guard to the steelworkers' union to the FBI, running around in a state of organized confusion as they directed the rescue and recovery efforts.

I met with some people from the Red Cross, and I stared at a wall of pictures. Everywhere, pictures of the missing were posted: friends, family members, husbands, sons, cousins. *Please Call*. I'd never seen anything like it. One flyer showed a picture of four kids, with a scratched crayon plea—*Daddy, please come home, we miss you*. I'd never expected to see such a thing, and I never want to again.

But what struck me most was the wishfulness of it. Even in the midst of that destruction, people were in a kind of determined denial, able to hope that a husband, or a wife, or a daughter would come walking through the door. In the face of the awful question—*If they're not at home and they're not in the hospital, then where are they?*—people chose to deny the worst and hope for the best.

The next morning was a Saturday, and it began early with a Red Cross rep taking us on a tour of firehouses. We started on the Lower East Side of Manhattan, and as I walked up to the first firehouse, I felt like a fool. I was an unannounced visitor, and maybe the firefighters didn't need one; maybe they had enough visitors. In front of the station there was a constant stream of well-wishers bringing food and gifts, leaving candles and murals behind. I worried that when I walked up, they'd say, "What the hell are you doing here? Get out of here."

I stepped inside the firehouse of Bowery Station 33, where they had lost 11 men from their unit. I stood there for a moment, not certain what to do. But then a firefighter recognized me. He said, "Fucking Lance Armstrong," like a true New Yorker, and then he hugged me, and he started to cry. Some more firefighters gathered around and we shook hands. "Nobody told us you were coming," they said.

One of them turned around and yelled to a guy who was sitting in the kitchen. He came out, and shook my hand, and I could tell he was heavily affected, maybe by the loss of his friends, or by what he had seen, or both. We talked for a bit, about what had happened, and what they had seen. They told me stories of the stench and the heat and the body parts everywhere.

The most troubled-seeming firefighter was a real cycling nut. One of his buddies said, "You guys should race." It turned out every station house kept a couple of bikes, old junkers, for errands. The firefighters spent long hours together in the firehouse kitchen, cooking and eating together, and whenever they needed more groceries, somebody jumped on the bike and went down to the store, threw all the stuff in the front basket and then pedaled back.

Somebody handed me a bike with big fat tires. I laughed and got on. The cycling nut jumped on his bike and started riding up and down the street, wanting to race, saying, "Come on, come on." One of his buddies said, "Look, he's having a really hard time. We're all having a hard time, but that guy is having a really hard one."

My friend the firefighter took off down the block, pedaling hard. He seemed so serious. It must have been a welcome escape, to get out there and sprint around on that bike. So I rode after him.

We were in the middle of a downtown street in New York City, surrounded by people and cars, but he was possessed. He mashed the pedals, while I chased him. We rounded a corner and headed back to the firehouse, and he beat me handily. All of the other firefighters whooped and clapped him on the back, and he broke into a huge grin.

I hung around for another thirty minutes or so, and then shook hands and went to the next firehouse.

We visited ten firehouses in all. Every one was the same, and I told Bart, "I could do this all day." They had big kitchens with long tables where firefighters and devastated family members sat around, mess-hall style. The chalk duty boards hadn't been changed: the date still read 9/11, and the names of the men were still posted. I don't know if they've changed them even yet. Outside, the firehouses were decorated with memorial candles, posters, and flowers, and crowds stood around thanking the firefighters, or just gazing, quiet and reverential, as if they were in a museum.

Some people think heroism is a reflex, an anti-death knee jerk.

Some people think heroism is a desire to matter, to be of use. Then there is the quieter heroism of "going to work every day and making a living for one's family," as New York mayor Rudolph Giuliani said of the people who died in those buildings. By the end of that trip I decided it was some combination of the three. But whatever it was, these guys had it.

Later that afternoon I was invited to meet with Giuliani. I was ushered into a command post, and he stood up and gave me a hug. Lying face-down on his table was a biography of Abraham Lincoln. Giuliani was exhausted, and deeply affected, but he was totally in control, obviously the perfect man for the job at that time. The mayor turned to another gentleman in the room, and introduced me: Bill Clinton. They invited me to ride with them in a helicopter tour of Ground Zero.

It looked like the entire lower part of Manhattan had turned into a junkyard. There was shredded metal scattered everywhere; shards of material had even been flung onto the tops of other buildings. There was no camera that could show the 360-degree perspective, the utter scope of the damage. The metal and broken glass glinted in the sunlight, and in the heart of Ground Zero itself, you could see the inferno, the forklike heap of wreckage smoldering, surreal. Some of the adjacent buildings had huge gouges taken out of them, as if a giant had dragged his finger through them. In one building, what must have been a 40-foot steel girder hung out of a window, as if it had been thrown like a spear.

Afterward, I went to a rest area where rescue workers—who had come from all over the country, as far away as Texas, California, and Ohio—were sleeping in rotations in a large warehouse, on cots. I sat and chatted with them, listening to their experiences. They had driven from across the country to help with the terrible job, and they were exhausted and shattered, and yet working around the clock. Mainly, they were angry. The *New York Post* had run a fold-out picture of Osama bin Laden with the caption WANTED DEAD OR ALIVE, and that thing was posted all throughout the building. That's when I realized we were in a war.

The salvage effort was an undertaking of backbreaking labor, and it changed my ideas about what real work was, because everything had been blown to smithereens, and the only people who knew what to do about it were the ones who could wield a jackhammer or drive a bobcat; the welders and grapplers and carpenters, doing a kind of work that many people aren't familiar with anymore. It was risky work, too, because each time they hoisted a piece of smoldering metal, something else fell, or burned. Broken glass showered on their heads, and the heaps of smoking junk literally burned the soles of their boots away, but they kept digging, first to find anyone alive, and then just to find anyone at all.

The posters fluttered from kiosks and restaurant windows and chain-link fences and concrete walls. Brothers sisters wives husbands cousins friends. New Yorkers wept in taxis, on trains, and sometimes they just stood still in the middle of the street and cried. Every day the rescue and recovery workers would pry up another giant piece of steel, exposing the core of fire, and another plume of smoke would shoot into the air. And everybody would feel the wreckage within their own hearts, a seemingly endless interior hemorrhage.

The last thing I did was go to Union Square, where I watched a candlelight vigil, and listened to some peace demonstrators. I respected their position, but I'd seen too much wreckage. I wanted to say, "My friend, fuck peace." It was difficult to feel charitable, diffi-

cult to summon anything but a deep, unpitying, unforgiving venge-
fulness, all of the most un-Biblical of sentiments. All you had to do
was go to a wall or a fence, and look at those pictures of the missing,
or go down to Ground Zero and smell that place. I was hard-pressed
to believe that God was in the air. Death was in the air—that was
death and burning that we smelled.

But good was there too, actual good, in the daily selfless acts of
digging performed by volunteers. The concrete was pulverized, the
steel was twisted, and in the midst of that a rescue worker would find
a child's toy, preserved. I didn't know what to make of that kind of
chance—or of the fact that the men who flew into those buildings
did so while praying.

One of the more interesting features of death is its deniability. It's
as if the human temperament has a built-in capacity to ignore its
own potential for nonexistence. How we can deny something so blaz-
ingly apparent, I don't know. But we do, maybe because we need to
in order to live productively from day to day. Otherwise we'd be so
stunned by the brevity of each second that we'd never go to work
and we'd all move to Tahiti.

I had been stripped of my capacity for denial, and now so were
New Yorkers. Talking to them was like talking to newly diagnosed
cancer patients. We shared the same sensations: of a dread diagnosis
and a hard new eye on reality. I was reminded again that survivorship
was an evolution: you had to learn to survive all kinds of things, not
just your own illness.

The strangeness of that period was complicated by the fact that my five-year cancer anniversary was coming up, and meanwhile the twins were due at any moment. Previously, I'd thought of the five-year anniversary as a big damn day. That was the day my doctors would say, "Okay, guy. See you later." Now it felt swamped by the enormity of what had happened in New York, and by the impending arrival of two new infants. Again, it came down to perspective: taxes, scandal, gossip, headache, traffic jams. It was all about separating the large from the small.

When my five-year checkup finally came, it was smaller than I'd imagined, an anticlimax. Kik stayed home, because by now she was in the seventh month of her pregnancy. Instead I flew to Oregon with Bill Stapleton, so we could combine the trip with a business meeting at the Nike headquarters. So one morning in the fall of 2001, I went to see Dr. Nichols at the Oregon Health Sciences University, in Portland, for my last cancer checkup.

I slouched in my seat on American Airlines, brooding and sick, and not getting better. The numbers weren't falling. By now the flight crew knew me. I was the bald guy, with no eyebrows or eyelashes and the skin that looked parched. The guy who looked like death—and who felt like it.

A flight attendant came down the aisle.

"How's it going?" he asked.

"You know what?" I said. "It's not going very well. It's not going well at all."

Even though I was on my way to my last checkup, it wasn't the end of cancer for me. I was surer than ever that cancer would always be with me, in terms of *other* people's cancer. It was there in the form of friends who were sick, friends who died: in the loss of my friend Stacy Pounds, and of my first great friend and benefactor in Austin,

J. T. Neal, and a little boy named Billy Rutledge, and a little girl I adored, Kelly Davidson.

Kelly had been diagnosed with neuroblastoma when she was in only the third grade. We'd met and bonded when we were both in remission, bald and fearful. We both needed physical action, and we both had smart mouths. I had gotten better, but she hadn't. The disease became increasingly hard to manage, but she kept trying.

I gave her a bike, and some Rollerblades, and we would go racing around together. She was indefatigable on them. She was the only person who could tell me what to do. "Are you coming over to ride bikes?" I asked her one day. "Yeah, and after that we're going fishing," she said.

But she got sicker. She underwent kidney surgery and had a tumor removed from her abdomen.

"You fight," I told her. "It hasn't beaten you, and it can't beat you. I don't let anything kick me without kicking back."

The kid who had threatened to zip away from her doctors and nurses on Rollerblades grew weak and needed a wheelchair. Soon she lost her hearing. First it was a matter of weeks, and then days. She entered a hospice, and failed rapidly.

I had called her from Europe shortly before the 2000 Tour. "Is there anything I can do for you?" I asked.

"Yeah, wear yellow for me," she had said.

Kelly died in August of 2000. Kik and I had tried to sort through the pending grief, tried to say the right things and be there the best we could, let her know how much we appreciated her. But when we lost her, we felt helpless and empty.

We were in Europe and couldn't get home, but my mother went to Kelly's funeral in our place, and read a letter from us. For the time being, our grief got cloistered, down the dark steps, padlocked, several layers below.

When we got back to Texas, we saw Kelly's family, but I couldn't think of the right things to say. I marveled at their strength. Kelly's mother, Jamie, got a job in medical research, and they launched a pediatric cancer foundation named for their daughter. One day Kik went with Jamie to see Kelly's gravesite. I couldn't make myself go. Kik described it: a peaceful spot under a lovely shade tree where people had placed flowers and little trinkets there for her. Luke and Kik put some flowers there for her, too—yellow, so she would know they were from us.

Not through my own choice, I was thrown into this cancer kinship, and for whatever reason, I survived, while there were legions of people who did not. Tests on a bicycle were flimsy compared with this sort of test, when something happened to somebody that you loved, and it called on you to be a stronger person than you were capable of being. All you could do was try to fortify yourself. But grief was inevitable, looming out there for all of us, sometime.

On the day of my final checkup, I rose early in my hotel room and drank the barium that would show up on the X rays and scans. Then I headed over to the medical center for the tests. Bill and my good friend from Nike, Scott MacEachern, went with me. They drank cups of coffee and chatted, while I put on a hospital robe and had a chest X ray and then an abdominal-pelvic CT scan. Dr. Nichols watched the readings to make sure nothing ominous was there, while Scott and Bill hung out with their coffees. Next, I gave blood so they could check for cancer markers.

The testing wasn't arduous, it was just a nuisance, and it only lasted an hour and a half or so. It was a box I was checking off, the last item on the long list. But it was evocative of everything I'd been through five years earlier: the sleeping 16 to 20 hours a day, and all the pills, and the logbook to keep track of what I was taking and when. All of the things I'd done to try to stay in front of the disease and educate myself, determined not to be helpless about my health. And it was evocative of what my ill friends went through every day.

Finally, Dr. Nichols did a last brief physical examination of me, going about his usual business in a clinical way. And then he was finished, and we sat down together.

"Your chances of ever having trouble with this again are in essence zero," he said. "You need to put this disease out of your mind, in terms of your own cancer."

I shook hands with Craig, and that was it, that was the big moment. I high-fived my friends and left that office for the last time. I called Kik and said, "All done." She started screaming and carrying on, and I just grinned.

When I got back to Austin, we had a party to celebrate the occasion. We had about 100 friends and family out to our future home site in the hills above Austin, the property we named Milagro, Spanish for "miracle." It was a cedar-studded expanse on a hillside, and I'd cleared a lot of the brush myself and had a small cabin built. I put in a huge rolling expanse of lawn for the kids, designed expressly for rolling down soft green hills, and I added a firepit, and dug out a dirt road.

For the party we put up strands of colored lights and built an outdoor stage for my friend Lyle Lovett, who performed, and after a while another of our good friends, Shawn (Sunny) Colvin, hopped up and joined him. Our friends spread blankets on the lawn and lounged, or fed themselves from a Mexican food buffet and drank margaritas. At the end of the evening I stood up, with Kik beside me, and thanked everybody for coming and remarked on how appropriate it was that we had named the property Milagro, because that's what it seemed to me, miraculous. Once, I'd wondered if I would live. Now it almost felt like cheating, to have been given my health and a whole life back, to have a healthy son like Luke, and twin girls on the way, and to be able to look at things with different eyes.

But the five-year mark wasn't the end of anything, not really. My story was encouraging for people who were beating cancer, but what about the people who weren't doing as well, who were flagging, and who lacked the energy to fight anymore? Who were losing ground, or not responding, or struggling to face something, whether the loss of a loved one in New York, or the next round of chemo?

I couldn't help them with the primary problem of surviving, and I couldn't change the basic biology of cancer. I couldn't help anybody. In the end, all I could do was try to encourage their attitude and will, try to talk about what cancer *couldn't* do.

It couldn't take away your spirituality, or your intelligence. It couldn't take away your love.

CHAPTER 5

Headwinds

When your value is constantly measured, and you're compensated for it, as an athlete is, you can get confused and start equating winning with a good and happy life.

The trouble is, nobody who does what I do for a living is happy-go-lucky. I don't bomb down a hill at 70 miles an hour with a smile on my face. If you want to win something, you've got to have single-mindedness, and it's all too easy to wind up lonesome while you're at it.

A race is an exercise in leaving others behind, and sometimes that can include the ones you love. It's a delicate problem, one I've yet to solve. For instance, one day I took my son bike-riding with me. I put him in a little trailer and hitched it to my bike, and we went pedaling off.

Luke said, out of nowhere, "No more airplane, Daddy."

"What?" I said, turning around.

"Daddy, no more airplane. Stay home with me now."

"Okay," I said. "Okay."

Spending life on the seat of a bike is a solitary exercise, and things go by in constant accelerated motion. Speed is a paradoxical equation: a thousand small, dully repetitive motions go into the act of going really, really fast, and you can get so fixed on the result, on the measurements and numbers and cadences, that you miss other things. Your strength as an athlete can be a weakness: the qualities that make someone fast don't always make them perceptive. Life becomes a blur.

Like every other season of my adult life, I entered the 2001–2002 cycling season with a sense of urgency, put there by cancer. When I wasn't trying to pedal faster on the bike, I was still trying to outrun the disease, and I focused on two sets of numbers, my pedaling cadence, and my blood markers, to tell me how I was doing. But maybe I missed some things, too.

That September, I had an irrational sense that the cancer was back. The battle with cancer is started and ended, and won and lost, on a cellular level, and I worried that the disease could lie dormant, hide out, and come back in ten years, or 20 years, just when I had strolled off into the sunset. I didn't ever want to disrespect the illness, or its track record. You could never turn your back on it.

I wasn't feeling well, and it made me uneasy. I was tired, and it wasn't from drinking unseemly amounts of beer, either, though that may have had something to do with it. I was stressed and physically exhausted from the long year, but I felt more than the usual fatigue. I was sleeping for 12 and 14 hours every night, long bouts of black, unconscious sleep. Monstrous sleep. It reminded me exactly of how I'd felt when I was sick.

The more I thought about it, the more I thought about it. I thought about it every hour.

Finally, I called my friend and general practitioner, Dr. Ace Alsup.

"Ace," I said, "I gotta come in for some tests."

"Why?"

"I just don't feel good. I'm nervous, and I don't want to be nervous."

"What do you want to do about it?" Ace asked.

"I want you to take my blood, and test it," I said. "I want blood tests, and I want them today. Please, call me the second you get the results, because I'm nervous as hell."

He said, "Okay. Come on down."

That afternoon, I slipped out of the house. I pocketed my keys and walked out the door without telling Kik. By now she was near the end of the pregnancy, and while she carried the twins with her usual grace, it couldn't be easy on her. I didn't want to worry her needlessly, didn't want to say to her, "Oh, I'm driving down to Ace's office for some blood work." I kept my worry to myself. Nothing else would reassure me—I just needed those numbers. So I made up some excuse about what I was doing that afternoon, and I snuck out.

I drove down to Ace's office, and he drew blood, and then I drove back home, and I sat by the phone. He promised he would call me as soon as he got the results. All I cared about was my HCG level, the critical blood marker for testicular cancer. HCG is a hormone that's perfectly common in pregnant women, but it shouldn't be present in more than trace amounts in a young man. If my HCG level was more than two, it would mean only one thing: the cancer was back. When it came to cancer, numbers were everything. All I wanted to know from Ace Alsup was that it was less than two.

When I was sick, my HCG skyrocketed. One morning, College called and asked how I was doing. I said, "The numbers went up." My HCG level was over 109,000. The cancer was spreading and now it was in my brain. My mother had spent the morning crying, but I was strangely relieved. College took me to lunch, to get me out of the house.

"I don't know why she keeps crying," I said. "I'm cool with this. At least now I know everything. Now I know what to do."

I sat there, alone, waiting for Ace Alsup to call back, and I asked myself what I'd do if the disease had returned. I told myself, *Okay, you've got a choice: you can give in . . . or fight like hell and hope to live forever.* When I was first sick, some doctors told me that my chances of living were 50 percent, some said 40 percent, and some said 20 percent. But one thing was for certain: any odds at all were better than 0 percent.

The phone rang. I picked it up—it was Ace.

"Just tell me it's less than two," I said. "If I hear that, I hang up the phone, and I'm done."

"It's less than two," he said.

I thanked him, and I hung up, and that was the end of it. But it wasn't the end of my unease on the subject.

I live with a constant sense of being pressed for time. I have to do everything *now*—get married, have children, win races, make money, ride motorcycles, jump off cliffs—because I might not have the chance later. It's an odd gift, that sort of concentrated living, and perhaps I don't always apply it to the right things. I'm either going at 150 percent, or I'm asleep.

When I get locked on to something, I don't hear, see, or notice anything around me. I hired a young Aussie guy named Christian

Knapp to be my training aide. Christian was a jack-of-all-trades, a masseur and physical trainer whose job was to help me work out, and accompany me on a motorbike when I went on long rides, to protect me from traffic. One spring afternoon we rode out together and spent seven hours on the bike, battling through a rainstorm. Toward the end of the day we finally came down, relieved, from the foothills into a beautiful green valley—and got hit by a sudden blast of wind, rushing straight into us. Chris idled next to me on the motorbike.

"Man, I bet you're bummed about this headwind," he said.

I looked at him.

"What headwind?" I said.

We spent that November in Austin, waiting out the last month of Kik's pregnancy peacefully; the twins were due right around December 1. But then, on the day before Thanksgiving, Kik went in for a routine checkup and mentioned to the doctor that she'd felt a little peculiar that morning. Dr. Uribe examined her briefly and said, "What's your husband doing today?" Kik replied that I was scheduled to leave for a series of business meetings.

"Well, you better call him to tell him to cancel the rest of his day, because you're having these babies. You need to go home and get a bag."

Kik called me, and said, "Can you cancel your meetings?"

"Uh, yeah," I said.

"Good. We're having these kids."

Kik drove home and walked in the door, and she said, "Pack our bags." We stood there and smiled at each other. It was the last time, Kik noted, that we would be together, just us, without being surrounded by children. We arranged for Luke to be picked up by his grandparents, and then, giggling with excitement, we threw some things into a suitcase. I was standing in the foyer holding the bags when the doorbell rang. I opened the door.

"Random drug control," the woman announced.

"You gotta be kidding," I said.

The lady thrust a piece of paper at me. "These are your rights."

I just stood there helplessly. "Ha," I said. I put down the bag.

She handed me the paper.

"You know what?" I said.

She stared at me.

"My wife is in labor. So it better be fast."

She gasped, and she whirled around to her male companion, who was still coming up the walk, and said, "Oh, my God, hurry up, hurry up."

But even in a hurry, the drug-testing procedure takes 15 to 20 minutes. I had to pee in a container, and then it had to be distributed into two other different containers, and the pH had to be tested, and then there was a bunch of paperwork to fill out. It seemed like there were 50 forms to get through. "Sign this form, and read this one," the lady said. I shoved the papers around and scribbled my name, while Kik stood there with her eyes wide and pleading, about to pop.

Finally, we got them out of the house, and I hustled Kik to the car and we drove to the hospital, and settled Kik into a room.

College met us there; we'd called him to tell him the good news. He had ordered his Tex-Mex lunch to go, and he brought it along with him. He settled into a couch in Kik's room and opened his lunch, and we chatted and ate chips and salsa. We teased College, who was a confirmed bachelor, and he teased us back. He called

Luke "The Seducer Child," because he claimed that Luke was the kind of kid who seduced you into wanting one of your own. College claimed, "If you don't want to have a baby, don't bring your girl-friend around Luke, because he's the kind who makes you think every kid is great. He grabs you by the hand, wants you to play with him or read him a book. And pretty soon the girl says, 'Honey, why don't we have one of those?' That Luke's a trouble kid. Keep your girlfriend away from that kid."

The smell of the food made Kik starving, because she wasn't al-lowed to eat anything all day to prepare for the birth. She said, "Come on, College, give me five chips. Just five." Finally he relented and dealt her out five chips.

Then a nurse came in, and told Kik to turn over. It was time for her epidural. The nurse prepared the long needle, and College didn't even know what it was. Kik said, laughing, "Hey, College, can you excuse me while I get this shot?" College jumped up like he'd been electrocuted and lunged into the hallway.

Then it was time to go to the delivery room, and I stayed next to Kik as we waited for our girls. The process of delivering twins was more involved and complicated than a single delivery, and there were lots of staff in the room—doctors, nurses, and neonatal specialists. This was more formal, more intense, and scarier, but in the end everything went smoothly, actually more smoothly than when Luke was born, in part because Kik was so brave and self-assured. She seemed to just push twice, and here they came, Grace Elizabeth at 8:54 P.M., and Isabelle Rose at 8:57.

Nothing has ever made me feel more alive than watching those children come into existence; the appearance of each of them was utterly momentous. Like Luke, they were true miracle babies, possible only through the marvel of IVF. I didn't care if they were girls or boys, large or small, blue-eyed or brown. All I cared about, and all I care about to this day, was that they existed, and were healthy.

I cut the umbilical cords, and cleaned them up, and we looked them over, beaming. Grace and Isabelle were instantly distinct to me, two very different little souls, though equally gorgeous. Later, it would puzzle me when other people had trouble telling them apart. How could anyone ever confuse the two? I wondered. Grace was slightly smaller and amazingly calm for a baby, and she seemed to accept kisses and adoration complacently, as if they were her due. Isabelle was the image of me, down to personality, just a tiny, wriggly version. She had small features and a kind of brightness in her eyes, and as she grew she would become a comical, almost antic baby. Right from the start we hardly ever called them by their full names. Grace was "Gee" or "Gracie" and Isabelle was "Izzy," or as Luke called her, "Isabo."

The next day was Thanksgiving, and we had dinner at the hospital, and it was awful—bad coffee, and warmed-up food, even re-circulated air—but we didn't care because we were so tired and happy. A day later, we brought the girls home and settled in, trying to adjust to a new schedule of dual feedings. Luke was instantly the warm, protective brother and wanted to play with the babies. I hired a night nurse to help Kik so she wouldn't be exhausted. The nurse brought the girls to her for middle-of-the-night feedings, and then took them back to the nursery while Kik grabbed some sleep.

One morning about a week after they were born, Kik and I were luxuriating in a quiet breakfast together when there was a knock on the door. We looked at each other, frustrated; it was only seven A.M., and all the babies were asleep, and we were drinking coffee in our bathrobes. There was another knock on the door, and the dog started barking. Kik and I were almost never alone. We both wanted to kill whoever was out there.

Kik opened the door.

"Random drug control," the woman said.

Kik couldn't believe it. "It's seven in the morning," she snapped.

The woman just stuck out the paperwork.

I came to the door.

"What are you doing?" I demanded.

"Random drug control," she repeated.

"Random? What's random about this? Are you kidding?"

Kik was so angry she was trembling. She'd always faintly resented the drug testers because of their lack of cordiality, the way they barged into the house and gave orders. "If only they'd say, 'How are you?'" she'd say. But this felt like an outright violation, for them to show up on the doorstep while we were in our bathrobes, with newborns in the house. They had seen Kik in labor, only a week earlier, and it had been all over the Austin paper when we brought the children home from the hospital, and they knew exactly how invasive a test must have been at this time in our lives. I was all for random testing, but this went too far. It felt like needless harassment in the game of "Gotcha."

For Kik, it was the worst possible time to see a stranger at the door. She was full of protective feelings for the babies and it was the last straw. There was just something about having them in our living room that felt wrong that day.

After I did the usual drug-test routine and paperwork, Kik

walked them to the front door. As they reached the threshold, Kik threw her arm out and blocked the way, so they couldn't leave. Kik leaned into the woman's face and said, through clenched teeth, "I don't want you coming over here early in the morning like this and disrupting this family *ever* again." But we both knew they'd be back.

We closed the door and went back inside and tried to resume our peaceful morning. But the moment was gone, and what no one could know was just how few of those moments there were. We didn't get very many of them.

Looking back on it now, the episode was telling. Life was a constant series of large and small disturbances, interruptions, breaks in the connection.

I was trying to oversee the renovating of our new apartment in Girona and the move from France to Spain, run a cancer foundation, and maintain a world-class cycling career all at the same time. But most important, we were parents to newborn twins, and to a two-year-old boy.

We lived in a rush—a focused rush, but a rush nonetheless—and sometimes we forgot the most basic things, with hilarious consequences. For instance, once I got Kik some real cycling gear, including a pair of high-performance shoes that clipped into the pedals. She trooped off to the gym and signed up for a spin class. She clipped herself into the bike, and worked out. When she got done, she popped off the bike—and couldn't figure out how to get the shoes off. She stared at the straps and buckles, baffled. I'd forgotten to show her how

In front of the entire gym, Kik had to clod-hop out the front door, down the stairs, and into the parking lot. She got into her car and drove home in the cycling shoes. I was sitting in the kitchen eating cereal when I heard, "clunk-clunk-clunk," coming down the hall.

"Why do you have your cycling shoes on?" I said.

"You have to help me take them off."

I burst out laughing.

The next day, Kik went back to the gym, and there was College, working out. Kik put on her cycling gear and got on a spin bike. College finished his own workout, and then wandered over to Kik.

"I just need to know if I have to hang around for another thirty minutes to help you out of those shoes," he said.

But we forgot some important things, too. For instance, we forgot to go to a quiet dinner, just the two of us. We breezed through the house, gave each other a kiss, a quick tackle, and then there was always something else to do, a baby that needed something or an important call.

Even in the off-season, I had to travel more than I liked, usually for the cancer foundation or to honor my endorsement contracts. I always tried to make it back home for dinner, but there were times when it was impossible. A typical week: I went to Europe for 48 hours for an appearance, and took the Concorde from Paris back to New York, changed planes, landed in Austin, and drove straight to a photo shoot. From there I went to sign books, jerseys, and posters for cancer survivors. Then I drove home, changed, and took a 35-minute bike ride. I showered, changed again, and spent some time with Kik and the kids. Then I changed yet again, and we went to a gala-fundraiser for the cancer foundation.

Meanwhile, Kik was bringing a similar energy to motherhood—

and a perfectionism, too. She didn't take the easy road. For instance, she didn't buy baby food; she wanted to give the kids real vegetables instead of processed stuff, so she cooked fresh ones and mashed them up.

We had help, in the form of a nine-to-five nanny and a house-keeper, but we still struggled to stay ahead of the game. I bought hours on a private plane, in order to get home at night and not miss too many of the struggles or highlights.

I'd walk in the door after being away, and Luke would launch himself at my stomach, and I'd feel a renewed surge of energy. I'd peer at Grace and Isabelle with a deep curiosity: each of them was changing daily. Soon Grace had outgrown Isabelle, and I wondered with a pang what else had happened without me.

Luke got a new two-wheeler from Trek, and he was so excited when he first saw it, he screamed "NEW BIKE, NEW BIKE!" He leaped on it and took off, ripping around the house and skillfully an-gling around furniture. I looked at Kik and said, "This is scary."

When he rode it outside for the first time, he crashed just like his father. Kik took him to a neighborhood with no traffic and smoothly paved streets. Luke was so excited that he wore his helmet the whole way over in the car. He jumped right on the bike and took off at top speed—with Kik chasing him. He took a sharp left and headed down-hill, and onto a cobblestoned driveway. He hit the bumps, and went flying headfirst from the bike and landed on his face. He got up bruised, scratched, and crying . . . but he just wiped his nose on Kik's shoulder and got right back on his bike. Just like his father.

I was deeply curious about parenting, and wanted to be a hands-on father. I didn't shy away from the responsibility. I respected and admired good fathers, most especially my father-in-law, Dave. I expected myself to be good at it, and felt devoted to the job—even when I wasn't sure how to go about it. I loved doing the small fatherly things—doting on the girls, taking Luke to school, talking to his teachers. The smallest act of fatherhood was very symbolic to me, and vital.

But I was discovering what a hard job it could be. Juggling three children all at once, plus meeting other responsibilities, was alternately joyful, chaotic, and overwhelming. There were so many small bodies and needs to attend to that I couldn't even find time to go to the bathroom.

One morning when the girls were still brand new, Kik was exhausted from handling three children with just two hands. I was out riding, and she was by herself. The twins went on dueling crying jags, and Luke was racing around being rambunctious.

Kik couldn't put a baby down long enough to answer the phone, or to get out of her pajamas. All of a sudden there was a knock on the door. Kik opened it, still in her pajamas and with an infant in each arm. It was her dad, Dave. "Hi, honey," he said. "I called and then I tried your cell phone, and you didn't answer either one, so I thought I would just stop in. I thought maybe you could use a hand."

"Bless you," Kik said. "Here, take a baby."

One afternoon I was out on my bike when my cell phone rang. It was David Millar, the great young British cyclist and my friend, calling from Paris. He was out on the town and had had a few drinks and decided to give me a ring.

"Please tell me you're not on your bike," he said.

"I'm on my bike."

"No! You bastard! It's December bloody first! How long have you been on it?"

"Three and a half hours."

"You bastard!"

If you asked me when I started preparing for the next Tour, my answer was, "The morning after." To my way of thinking, the Tour wasn't won in July, it was won by riding when other people weren't willing to.

That meant there was no such thing as an off-season. I rode year-round. In a way, I preferred training to my other responsibilities. Since I wasn't in the States very much, there was always too much to do, people to see, requests to fulfill. It was actually a relief when the cycling season resumed each February and we returned to Europe.

From then on I trained with a meditative concentration on my job. It was isolating, but it was also an escape, with no distractions and fewer potential problems. It simplified everything.

This year, I looked forward to going back to Europe and having some peaceful time with my family, because our new home in Girona was finally ready.

The result was breathtaking. What had been a dank, crumbling old set of rooms was now a large, gracious apartment. The floor-to-ceiling terraced windows were hung with rich magenta drapes, and the ancient columns had been repainted with gilt. In a small cloistered garden, a fountain burbled beneath 12th-century stonework arches and cornices. My friend and architect Ryan Street had turned it into a four-bedroom family home with every modern comfort and fixture, while preserving the atmosphere and detail of the old rooms. The chapel was splendid, and even a set of broken-paned stained-glass doors under gothic arches had been restored. Hanging over the altar was the beautiful piece of religious art I'd found for Kik, a 15th-century crucifixion scene painted on wood.

Back home, the girls needed passports. Luke already had one, with his tiny baby photo on it. He was screaming at the time it was taken, so his face in the photo was a red "O," and even the frowning Frenchmen in customs smiled when they saw it.

I wanted to make it as easy as possible for Kik to travel with the children and the cat-and-dog menagerie, so I booked a private charter flight for them. Rather than hassle with changing planes and trying to get through customs with a double stroller, as she usually did, Kik and the kids went to a private terminal and flew direct from Austin to Girona in a little over eight hours. It was the best I could do under the circumstances. Still, we'd have both preferred it if I had been there to help.

I was already in love with Girona, a city that was once conquered by Charlemagne and then later reclaimed by the Moors. I never tired of strolling down the elegant arcades, or stopping at the gothic cathedral, behind which were ruins and improbable gardens planted through the different ages.

Kik walked into the apartment to find that all of our things had arrived from France and every piece of furniture and dish was in place. Her reaction was what I'd hoped: she looked around the huge, high-ceilinged rooms and pronounced them "palatial." It was a far cry from her move several years earlier, with a mattress tied to the top of a Renault.

Kik loved the history and elegance of the old town center of Girona, with its arched stone doorways and cobbled streets. She had never lived in an urban setting before, so it was a new experience for her to ride a private elevator one flight down to the ground floor, and to walk a couple of blocks to do her shopping. She wandered through the Ramblas, the main pedestrian square, ducking into the various specialty shops for bread, or tea, or seafood. Or, she could just order groceries over the Internet and have them delivered to the door.

That spring we had a baptism for Grace and Isabelle, now almost six months old, in the Girona cathedral. We stood in the ancient baptismal nave, in the evening, surrounded by Kik's family and some friends. The priest conducted the ceremony in Spanish, and at one point as he gestured with his hand, Luke thought he wanted to shake. Luke walked right up and took his hand in the middle of the ceremony. We all laughed, the priest included.

The apartment was near the Ramblas, which made it easy for Kik to load up the double stroller and wheel it through the center of town. We bought Luke a little skateboard that attached to the back of a stroller, so he could ride along behind the girls. Luke made himself at home in Spain, which was no surprise. He said "*hola,*" and "*gracias,*" and "*hasta luego*" to everyone, charming his way to free cookies and other items. But he was unmistakably American in his Nike duds and a backwards cap that said UNIVERSITY OF TEXAS.

A typical day: I rose at about seven A.M. for coffee, and read the paper, and if something interrupted the ritual, I was grumpy. Next, I dealt with the overnight e-mails and fired off business correspondence. Sometimes, Bill Stapleton arrived at the office to find as many

as 20 messages from me by nine A.M. Breakfast depended on my training and how many calories I would burn that day: sometimes fruit,
sometimes muesli, sometimes egg whites and fresh bread. Then I left
home on my bike to train for anywhere from three to seven hours.

After I got home, I showered, ate some pasta, and returned more
phone calls and e-mails, and then lay down for a nap. While I slept,
Kik made dinner, usually fish or chicken and steamed vegetables.
When I woke up, I played with the kids and had dinner. In the
evening, we read or watched television, and we were all in bed by ten
P.M. That was it. And we did it every day, for months on end.

Outwardly, Kik seemed content with our lives. When I came
home from riding, there was pasta or soup boiling on the stove, the
kids would be adorable and happy, and she always said she'd had a
good day. She rarely complained or balked at the intensity of my
training or the solitude of her own life in Europe, away from her parents and friends. I could have said, "I need to eat grass for dinner and
go to bed at six," and she'd have said fine, and help me do it. She was
sunny-natured and she kept negative air out of the house. We almost
never fought.

But in retrospect, perhaps we should have. For the first few years
together, it was an adventure for both of us to live the life of a European cyclist. But over time, it became less of an adventure, and
now with three children it began to mean spending stretches of time
apart. It was just too hard to move three children around, and we
weren't willing to leave them with a nanny.

We no longer went places together the way we once had. In
March, I left for a one-day race, Milan–San Remo, an event she'd always come to in the past. But this time she stayed home in Girona. I
flew to Milan alone, and raced 300 kilometers, and afterward I threw

on dry clothes, sped to the airport and flew home. I made it back in time for dinner. I was aching with fatigue, but I was home.

It was the rain that made Floyd Landis drink 13 cappuccinos.

It wasn't because he thought it was a good idea.

Floyd and another young member of the U.S. Postal team, Dave Zabriskie, were sharing an apartment in Girona in the spring of 2002, and it had rained for weeks on end. There wasn't a lot to do except ride their bikes, and it had strained their abilities to entertain themselves. When they woke up to gray skies and wet streets for yet another day, Floyd said to Dave, "Screw it, let's not ride today. Let's hang out at the café."

They wandered down to the town square and took a table in a sidewalk café. They watched people go by, and Floyd ordered a cappuccino. It arrived, frothing and aromatic. After a while, he ordered another, and then another. "How many of those are you going to drink?" Zabriskie said. Floyd shrugged. So Zabriskie joined him, and ordered another. And it went on like that for three hours, Floyd and Dave lounging and drinking coffee, after coffee, after coffee, with mounting hilarity. When the check came, Floyd found he'd had 13 cappuccinos.

The next day the story got back to me. I'd been watching Floyd carefully. He was an interesting new kid on the team, made up of equal parts mischief and talent. He was a 26-year-old from a Mennonite family in Lancaster, Pennsylvania, who'd run off to become a mountain biker and had then switched over to road racing. He showed promise, but he'd had some hard luck, and he obviously hadn't yet learned how to be a professional, either. He was loud and smart-alecky and he liked to blast ZZ Top, which in combination with his iffy training habits made him seem like a slacker to the veteran cyclists on our team, who were all serious in their work habits. If he didn't know better than to blow off training and try to give himself caffeine poisoning, he needed to learn. Mainly he was young.

I called him up. "Floyd, what are you doing tomorrow?"

He said, "Oh, I'm going to do a two-hour ride with the guys."

I said, "No, you're not. You're going to do five hours with me and we're going to have a little talk."

He met me the next morning, and we rode into the hills above Girona, and I told him I'd heard what he had done.

"Man, you *cannot* act that way," I said. "You can't treat your body that way, you can't train that way, and you can't treat your teammates that way."

Floyd was very open, and apologetic. He said, "I know, I know."

"Look man, you gotta get it together," I said. "You've got to have a little balance. You aren't born a professional. You have to turn yourself into one. You have to do the right things. You have to eat right. You have to sleep right."

I knew that Floyd was in the midst of a hard year. His previous cycling team, Mercury, had gone bankrupt when a sponsor pulled out, and Floyd only got paid half of what he was owed, and he was out of racing for eight months. Eventually, he got up the nerve to contact Postal and ask if he was wanted, and we said sure. Now he was one of 20 riders on the Postal roster, and he had a chance to be one of the nine riders selected by Johan to ride in the Tour—if he worked hard.

But Floyd was distracted. He was loaded down with debt, because he'd maxed out his credit cards when his team folded. He had medical and dental bills, and was struggling to support his family, his wife, Amber, and his six-year-old daughter, Ryan. He didn't know what to expect from his new team, or what was expected from him in return, or even whether he had a future as a rider.

"Look, pal," I said, "you've got to get this right. Listen to me, and do what I tell you."

I explained the math: Floyd was making a salary of $60,000, but if he bore down and made the nine-man squad that raced in the Tour, and we won, he would get about $50,000 more in prize money. "And then I'm going to throw a Lance-bonus on top of it," I said. "But to do it, you've got to focus, and quit worrying about anything else. Your family, debt, money, stress, you have to forget all of it. You've got to focus on this one thing."

Floyd said that was easier said than done.

"Forget it," I repeated. "You just fucking ride your bike."

But the very advice I was giving Floyd—to focus on cycling to the exclusion of all else—was the subject about which I struggled most. I constantly considered the cost of a career as demanding as cycling, versus the demands of a young family. How to balance the two? One of the ways in which I was determined to be a good father was to make the best living I could for them, make the most out of this brief opportunity I had as a world-champion athlete. But professional success could become a personal failure, if cycling came at the expense of our family.

In Floyd's case at the time, it was the right choice, and the only one. There aren't many clearly marked, signpost moments in your life, but occasionally they come along, and you have a choice. You can either do something the same old way, or you can make a better decision. You have to be able to recognize the moment, and to act on it, at risk of saying later, "That's when it all could have been different." If you're willing to make a harder choice, you can redesign your life. This was Floyd's moment, when he could change everything for himself, and I wanted him to know it.

Floyd agreed, and for the next several weeks, we trained together. He went with me to St. Moritz for altitude training. We went on reconnaissance rides for the Tour stages. We rode together for hours on end, and he learned, on a day-to-day basis, what I meant by professionalism. He learned focus, the ability to ignore large distractions, and to concentrate on the process. He learned resolve.

Sometimes others see more ability in you than you see in yourself. As a young rider, I'd been something like Floyd, a talented thrasher who didn't know how good he could be. What was true in his case had once been true in mine: I'd been ambitious but directionless, and a little bit of a loudmouth American, until older riders taught me better.

I'd never conceived of the Tour de France as a race I was capable of winning before Johan Bruyneel told me I could. I remember the moment when he said it to me, back in 1998. Johan was the newly named director of the Postal team, and I was the newly named team leader, and while I'd begun to work my way back from illness, I was still a tentative rider. I'd recently placed fourth in the Tour of Spain, a three-week road race, and Johan had watched me closely.

I was about to ride in the World Championships in Holland when Johan came to see me in my hotel room. He immediately started to talk about his ambitions for me and the Postal team.

"Okay," he said, "you just took fourth in Spain, without any special preparation, without having trained for it. You just showed up, you didn't even have the ambition to be in the top five, and you ended up fourth. So I think next year we have to work toward the Tour de France."

"Yeah, okay," I said. "I can win some stages."

"No, no, to win the whole thing," he said.

I stared at him, doubtfully. I was just glad to be there, to have a bike and a job again. I said, "Well, yeah, right. Look, I'm thinking about the World Championships now. We'll talk about this later."

Johan let the topic go for the moment, but he came back to it a couple of days later. Traditionally, the winner of the World Championships wears a rainbow-colored jersey for the entire year, signifying that he is the title-holder. Just before I raced, Johan wrote me an e-mail. "Good luck," he said. "I think you will look great on the podium of the Tour de France in the rainbow jersey."

I didn't win the Worlds—I was fourth. But the idea of winning the Tour began to grow in me.

Johan knew me more by reputation than anything else: a huge talent who didn't get everything out of himself. Every once in a while, I'd deliver a big ride: when I was 21, I had come out of nowhere to win the Worlds, and then a stage of the Tour de France. But mostly I cruised for months at a time, performing decently but not exceptionally, just barely meeting the definition of "professional."

Back then, I thought I was doing all that I could do. After the cancer, I realized I'd been operating at about half of my abilities. The truth was that I'd never trained as hard as I could, never focused as much as I could.

For one thing, I carried around 15 to 20 pounds more weight

than I should have, some of it in puppy fat and some of it in margaritas and tortilla chips. After cancer, I was 20 pounds lighter.

Under Johan, I began training seriously, and kept the weight off, and discovered what a huge difference it made in the mountains, where your own body was your biggest adversary. The lost weight, I discovered, made me 10 to 12 minutes faster over a mountain stage; I figured it saved me about three minutes on every mountain pass I rode.

Also, I began to work on becoming an efficient rider. As a young rider, I would start off at the gun, and just go. I didn't really know how to race—I mashed big gears and thrashed around on the bike, my position all wrong. Now, with Johan and Chris Carmichael, I studied proper aerodynamic positioning and effective cadence. Instead of cranking a big gear without much technique, I used a smaller gear and quicker pedal strokes as I moved uphill. I became an extremely good technical rider—the athlete turned into a trained and practiced cyclist.

There was no mystery and no miracle drug that helped me win that Tour de France in 1999, I explained to Floyd. It was a matter of recognizing the moment. It was a matter of better training and technique, and my experience with cancer and subsequent willingness to make the sacrifices. These were the explanations. If you want to do something great, you need a strong will and attention to detail. If you surveyed all the greatly successful people in this world, some would be charismatic, some would be not so; some would be tall, some would be short; some would be fat, some would be thin. But the common denominator is that they're all capable of sustained, focused attention.

Since then, I'd become ever more fixated on the Tour de France, both as a personal challenge and an objective one. The race became not so much about beating others, but about turning the competition against myself. I was obsessed with doing it a little better than I had before, a little bit better than last year, or last month, or even yesterday.

The Tour is essentially a math problem, a 2,000-mile race over three weeks that's sometimes won by a margin of a minute or less. How do you propel yourself through space on a bicycle, sometimes steeply uphill, at a speed sustainable for three weeks? Every second counts.

You had to be willing to examine any small part of your body or the bike to find extra time, I told Floyd; to look for fractions of seconds in something as small as the sleeves of your jersey. "Once you reach a certain level, everyone is good, and everyone trains hard," I said. The difference is who is more meticulous, willing to find the smallest increments of time, and as you get older and more experienced, the percentage gains grow smaller and smaller.

You had to become a slave to data, to performance indicators like pedal cadence, and power output measured in watts. You had to measure literally every heartbeat, and every morsel you ate, down to each spoonful of cereal. You had to be willing to look like a vampire, your body-fat hovering around three or four percent, if it made you faster. If you weighed too little, you wouldn't have the physical resources to generate enough speed. If you weighed too much, your body was a burden. It was a matter of power to weight.

Who knew when you might find a winning margin in a wind tunnel in December, during equipment testing? You might find another fraction of time in your position on the bike, or in a helmet, or in the composition of a wheel. Aerodynamics are different for every type of road, and for mild pitches, steep climbs, and long grades, so I worked on strengthening my hip flexors and my lower back, until I could hold certain positions—because the smallest thing, like moving your hands on the handlebars, could make you three seconds slower over 25 miles. I practiced changes in rhythm, accelerations.

I drove Trek's advanced-concept group crazy with testing new equipment, always looking for fractions of seconds. I wanted the bike lighter, I wanted it more aerodynamic, I wanted better wheels. I could lift a carbon-fiber frame with one finger, but I asked, "Can't you make it even lighter?" A tiny change in the weight or construction of the bike could save 10 to 15 seconds over the course of a 24-mile time trial. We played with computer-assisted design, aerospace materials. A hydration system was installed, so I could sip fluids without having to shift on the bike from the ideal aerodynamic position—it might save me another 10 seconds.

I tinkered with the bike incessantly. I was always changing the seat height, or the bars, a little down, or up. I talked to engineers, became personally acquainted with every pipe and tube. I'd become so attuned to the bike that I could sense the slightest alteration, like the princess and the pea. A mechanic might change my seat by a micrometer.

"Who messed with my bike?" I'd say.

When I was in remission, College and I took a driving tour of Europe. We rented a Renault, and I drove it so fast and so hard, I did something to the engine. When I floored it, it developed a faint high-pitched whining sound, Wheeeeeeeeeeee.

Finally, on our way from Italy to Switzerland, I got tired. I let College take the wheel, but only if he promised to keep his foot down on the accelerator.

"Put it to the floor," I instructed him.

I dozed off in the passenger seat. When he was sure I was fully asleep, College eased off the gas. The Wheeeeeeeeee *slowed to a* Waaaaaaaaaaah.

My eyes snapped open. "Put it to the floor," I said.

The winning is really in the details, I told Floyd. It's in the details that you get ahead. And in racing, "If you aren't getting ahead, you might as well be going backwards," I said.

The data and the numbers and the details gave you a psychological edge, not just physical. Each time I rode a hard climb twice, I told myself I was doing something no one else had done; that nobody in the Tour had suffered and worked as hard as I had. It gave me a deeper overall strength.

The reason we trained in bad weather, I told Floyd, was because a race wouldn't be cancelled just because it was 40 degrees and sleeting. Unless you ride in the cold you can't know how it feels, can't understand the sensation of cold seeping into your legs and stiffening them. That was a kind of strength you could only acquire by riding in it.

We spent most of May off in the mountains, training, and we rode at such high elevations that we got snowed out.

One day as I was riding, Johan pulled up next to me and said, "There's snow six kilometers from the top, you can't get through the pass."

"How much snow?" I asked.

"From an avalanche," he said.

"What if I keep going?"

"You can't."

"Who says?"

That's what it took to win the Tour.

One day I rode to a huge mountain called La Plagne. I reached the top after six and a half hours, then descended. At the bottom I just turned the bike around and went up again. I finished with more than eight hours of riding that day. It was dark when I got off the bike.

Nobody could give that kind of confidence to an athlete, except himself. It couldn't be faked, or called up at the last minute. You got it from everything you did leading up to the competition, so that on the day of the race itself, you looked around at all the other strong riders beside you, and said, "I'm ready. I've done more than they have. Bring it on."

But these things didn't always make me easy to work with. Johan Bruyneel and Chris Carmichael got 100 percent from me, and I wanted 100 percent from them. I called Johan four and five times a day.

I've been known to call Carmichael at one A.M. and say, "What are you doing?" If he hadn't posted my latest training program to me via e-mail, I wanted to know why not.

"Why isn't it up? You said you'd get it done."

"I forgot."

"You forgot? What do you mean you forgot? What if I forgot to show up at the Tour?"

"I'll get it done," Chris said. And he'd get up, while I was on the phone, and go to his computer.

"Listen," I'd say, "at this time last year my cadence was 93, and now it's 90, but I'm at the same wattage. How come? We need to look at that, and the spreadsheets of my last twelve tests, and measure them against where I was two years ago . . ."

A bike race was a comparatively easy and compelling form of success. There was a surety to the math: I knew within a fractional certainty how I would perform in a race because it had all been measured. It was ultimate, total confidence in the data.

But matters like marriage, or moving, or parenting, were more complicated and ambiguous compared to winning a race. In May, Kik and I celebrated our four-year wedding anniversary. We had a rare dinner out in Girona, just the two of us. Date night for us was becoming a once-a-year deal, on a birthday or our anniversary.

It was an occasion for reminiscing. Kik and I had first met when I was recovering from cancer and didn't yet know what I would do with the rest of my life, or how much of a life I would have. She was working for a marketing agency that promoted the cancer founda-tion, and she hassled me about not doing more for a corporate spon-sor. We ended up having a drink to make peace—and from then on, we spent all of our time together. I'd known women who were smart, or pretty, or funny, but until Kik I hadn't met one who was so many things all at once.

Dave Richard hadn't liked any of Kik's boyfriends. He shot every one of them down. Finally, she said, "Dad, am I ever going to find anybody to satisfy you?" Dave knew then that he had better try to like the next one. "I'm out of ammo," he said to his wife. The next guy she brought home was me. She invited me to her parents' in Rye, New York for Christmas, and by then I was already thinking of pro-posing, and hoping she would accept. After the holiday, I sent Kik's mother, Ethel, an e-mail thanking her. I added, "You've raised a wonderful daughter." Ethel wrote me back and said, "Thanks for the nice compliment, but are you sucking up?" I wrote back, "If it's working, I'm sucking." I proposed to Kik after just four months.

At our anniversary dinner, we realized all that we'd done since that time: we'd had four residences and three children, a bunch of bike-wrecks and various medical checkups, and we'd been through three Tours. We'd done it all fast. We fell in love fast, got married fast, had children fast, had success fast, and had more children fast. But we were about to have problems fast.

From the outside it looked graceful and easy, a golden, storybook life, and often it was. But there was a growing tension between appearances, what the rest of the world expected us to feel, and what we were actually feeling. The reality was that at the end of the day, we were like everybody else. The kids were tired and hungry, and the adults were, too. I'd walk through the door, physically spent. Kik would be worn out from a day with three small children under the age of three. It didn't help that neither of us wanted to admit to problems or fatigue or the threat of slippage—we weren't supposed to experience everyday unhappiness, because we'd been given so much. Neither one of us was able to say to the other, "This doesn't feel quite right." So we simply drifted on, doing our best.

A far more difficult test of endurance than a bike race is how you handle the smaller, common circumstances of your days, the more mundane difficulty of trying to make your life work. It's a typical assumption that the lessons of athletic competition are transferable. But the truth is that sometimes they are, and sometimes they aren't.

How do you measure whether you're being a good mate and a consistent parent? If other versions of success aren't as clear-cut as a bike race, frankly, they're also harder to come by. They can't be measured with data. They also provide an immeasurable satisfaction.

I was a beacon of survivorship—but I wasn't immune to its effects, and one of the emotional traps of survivorship is a *rush* to happiness. You race toward joy, exhilarated, and tell yourself that you don't have a moment to waste on anything that feels wrong or un-pleasant. "Why am I doing this?" I'd say. But a rush to happiness is impossible to achieve. Pure happiness is a rope slipping through your fingers, a silky sense of something passing from your grip. It's re-placed by exigencies, hard work, renewals, chores, obligations, and another day.

CHAPTER 6

Blue Train (*Le Train Bleu*)

Picture it: two hundred riders flying down a narrow road at 45 miles an hour, all of them trying to ride in front, bumping, jostling, punching, cutting each other off, and even jumping curbs in an effort to get ahead. Some of them will leave tire tracks on your back, if you let them. It's just one of the ways in which the Tour de France accurately imitates real life.

It takes eight fellow U.S. Postal Service riders to get me to the finish line in one piece, let alone in first place. Cycling is far more of a team sport than spectators realize, and it's an embarrassment worth cringing over that I've stood on the podium of the Tour de France alone, as if I got there by myself. I don't just show up there after almost three thousand miles, and say, "Look what I did." When I wear the yellow jersey, I figure I only deserve the zipper. The rest of it, each sleeve, the front, the back, belongs to the guys.

The Tour de France poses an interesting question about the nature of teamwork: why should eight riders sweat and suffer for three weeks when only one man, me, will get the trophy? This is asking for an extreme degree of self-sacrifice, perhaps even an unnatural amount. But the smart athlete, and person, knows that if self-sacrifice is hard, self-interest is worse. It dooms a team; you wind up a bunch of singletons that just happen to wear the same shirts.

A great team is a mysterious thing, hard to create, much less duplicate, and there are a lot more bad teams in the world than good ones. Just look around. Many groups who go through hardships together *don't* bond—all you have to do is survey the NFL, the NBA, and corporate America to see that. People talk about teamwork all the time: it's a shopworn and overused term, experts try to explain and define it, charlatans write books on the subject, but few really understand it.

And no wonder: teammates have an odd relationship; they float somewhere between acquaintances and relatives. But I contend that people are meant to work together in groups, not alone, and that a certain amount of self-sacrifice is not unnatural, but natural. Think about it: people have been gathering together in group efforts throughout time.

If you truly invest yourself in a team, you guarantee yourself a return on your investment, and that's a big competitive advantage over other less-committed teams. On the Postal Service team, we invest in each other's efforts—and the result is that we often have the sensation that we're racing against teams that merely spend themselves. What's smarter, to invest or spend? Investment implies a longer-term commitment; it's not shallow or ephemeral; it's enduring, and it suggests a long-term return.

There have been times when I've practically lived out of the same suitcase with George Hincapie. In cycling we're on the side of a mountain for weeks, in small hotel rooms, sharing every ache, and pain, and meal. You get to know everything about each other, including things you'd rather not.

For instance, I know that George has such heavy stubble on his chin that he has to shave about every hour. I learned that one August when we roomed together on the road. One morning, George was in the bathroom shaving, when I heard him yell.

"God*dammit*. It happened again!"

I went running toward the bathroom. "What happened?"

He stepped around the corner, beaming and clean-shaven.

"I just got better-looking," he said.

You can't always tell what makes a good team—but you know one when you see it, because the team members like each other. Sometimes we'll stay at a hotel where two or three other teams are lodged, and we all end up in the dining room together. Our Postal team sits around the table laughing, and chucking dinner rolls, and even after we're done we linger over our plates, enjoying each other's company. But across the aisle is a team that's full of free agents, with no one working very hard in anyone else's behalf. They eat with their heads hanging down over their plates, not making conversation, and as soon as they finish their meals, they go to their rooms. And in a pack sprint to the finish line, a solo rider without allies or associates is a tired and losing one.

The 2002 U.S. Postal Service team was one of the best cycling teams that ever rode a road. What made the personalities of nine different men on bikes meld into a single agreeable entity? Reciprocity is the answer. Too many people (especially bosses) demand or try to foster teamwork without grasping its most crucial aspect: a team is just another version of a community. The same principles apply to any communal undertaking, whether you're talking about a community garden, a neighborhood watch, or racing around France: if you want something, first you have to give it. You have to invest in it.

If I don't want to get sideways with the guys on my team, it's important to make them feel that when I'm winning, they are, too. One way to do so is to ride on their behalf in several races a year. I spend a portion of each spring working as a support rider and trying to help my teammates win races. I act as a domestique, shield them from the wind, protect them in the pack, and carry their water bottles—and it's one of my favorite parts of the season. And you know what? It *feels* good. I don't just do it so that they'll do the same for me in the Tour de France. I also do it because it feels better than solitude, it's more gratifying than riding purely alone.

The 2002 USPS team was made up of like-minded riders. By that I don't mean that we agreed on politics, or music. We simply shared an ethic. The reason we did so was that Johan and I had spent the previous five years carefully identifying, recruiting, and signing the kind of people we wanted to work with. Cycling is a free-agent world: it's a sport full of riders who will subtly hold back, and ride for themselves rather than the team, with only their own contracts in mind. We didn't have room for that. We'd had riders on the team we suspected of feeling that way—and they weren't on the team anymore.

Over the years, other riders had come and gone simply because they were so good that they were lured away to lead their own teams. Free agency makes it doubly difficult to form a cohesive team, because the personnel changes regularly from year to year, and 2002 was no exception: Tyler Hamilton, who'd helped me to three Tour victories, was stolen away from us to lead a Danish squad. (He remained a good friend and close neighbor.) But hopefully all of our riders, present and future, are of a type, committed to the team strategy and to doing the small things right.

At the start of each season we started training with 20 USPS riders from all over the world. Various factors went into selecting the nine team members who would take the start line in the Tour de France, including who was riding well at that time of year, and what roles they could fill—we needed some climbers, we needed some guys for the flats, and we needed domestiques—but what mattered most was how much they were willing to sacrifice. If you weren't thinking "team," you got left home. It was that plain.

We called it Dead Man's Rules. If you violated the ethic, broke the rules, crossed the line, you were off the team. Everybody went into the Tour knowing there was no self-interest. It was all-team, or all-nothing. If a guy wasn't thinking this way, then we didn't want him, not even if he was one of the best riders in the world, because it wasn't a good fit for us. That didn't always make us the best of friends with people outside the organization—I was viewed by some as a cold-blooded tyrant. I didn't talk much to other riders. If you weren't on the Postal team, I wasn't a social butterfly.

We wanted riders who rode with 100 percent aggression. The Postal formula to prepare for the Tour was simple: measure the weight of the body, the weight of the bike, and the power of the legs. Make the weight go down, and the power go up. We watched our diet, were consistent in training habits, and went over every inch of the course. (You'd think every team would do it, but they don't.) We didn't accept slacking—you have to know that everybody is working as hard as you are—but we encouraged good humor, because we believed it was excellent painkiller. You had to mix laughs with the hard work, and be able to tease each other without getting offended.

A couple of weeks before the 2002 Tour, Johan named the nine who would be on the start line. Each rider would have to play a different role and serve a different need over the various stages of the race. But their main job was to keep everybody out of the winner's circle but me.

The team:

George Hincapie was a dryly funny man and one of the most accomplished men in American cycling. He was true-blue, like a brother to me, solid and serious about his professional responsibilities every day. Nothing ever seemed to faze George, or his chronic wit—not even the hardest stage of the Tour.

I described George's style as "fingers in the nose." You could see other people breathing hard, with their mouths hanging open, gasping for air through their ears, through their eyes, through their pores. But even when George was in a full sprint, you never saw his nostrils flare. It was as though he didn't need to breathe, didn't even have to use his nose. That was George, fingers in the nose.

Victor Peña (Colombia), Pavel Padrnos (Czech Republic), and Benoît Joachim (Luxembourg) were consummate Tour domestiques, professional cyclists who could and did win different types of races around the world, but who for three weeks were willing to subjugate their efforts to the peculiar job of the world's longest stage race, for the sheer honor of the thing. They were formidable, stone-faced, and hard-bodied, and some people were afraid to talk to them because of how they looked, but the truth is, they were big teddy bears who gave of themselves every day and always looked for a way to help. They protected me from 200 other riders who wanted to beat up on me, guarded me against crashes and sideswipes, chased down breakaways, ferried food and water, sheltered me from the wind. The longer they could stay in front of me, the fresher my legs would be at the end.

I liked to say of my old friend Viacheslav Ekimov, the Olympic champion, that he was nails. Meaning, "hard as." He never complained, never whined, always delivered. We'd rather have his ethic on the team than some million-dollar talent who only rode hard when he felt like it.

Ekimov had retired at the end of the 2001 season, but he already missed cycling. He called Johan in February, when we were in a training camp in Europe, and said he wanted to race again, and he asked if there was still a place for him. "For you there's always a place on the team," Johan said. Eki started training, but we figured he wouldn't be race-ready until after the Tour. Typically, he showed up in early May at training camp, race-fit, the most in-shape of any of us.

Johan watched him for a few days, and said, "Eki, what do you think of the Tour de France this year?"

"What about it?" Eki said.

"Would you like to do it?"

"Yeah, I would love to do it."

"Well, you have no choice. You have to do it. We need you."

From then on, Ekimov was one of our freshest riders. He had the mentality of a junior, excited to be there again, and happy every day that he was on the bike.

Roberto Heras and José Luis "Chechu" Rubiera were young Spaniards with beautifully civilized manners, but on bicycles they climbed mountains with leg-breaking intensity. Heras was slightly-built and reserved, but when he was on the bike scaling an alp he seemed to flutter with a hyperkinetic, hummingbird quality. He was so good that there were times when I had trouble keeping the pace he set.

Chechu was an easy laugher, one of the more gregarious and well-loved men on the team, but he had his serious side, too. He was an engineering student who brought his textbooks on the team bus. Both of these guys gave of themselves on every ride, no matter how sore or banged up they were. They never held back, or seemed to have an off day. Or a bad mood, either.

Then there was Floyd Landis. One afternoon we were out riding together, and I said, "Who do you think we should pick for the Tour?"

"Well, obviously, I'm going to say me," he said.

I laughed. Then I named our seven top riders. I finished up by saying, "And, obviously, you."

Floyd almost jumped off his bike with excitement. "Really? Really?"

"If things keep going the way they are," I said.

The last big tune-up race before the Tour was called the Dauphiné Libéré. I won it—and Floyd got second. It was the first time Floyd had done anything in a European race, a huge result for a novice, and it was obvious he was the right choice for a teammate. I patted myself on the back for being smart enough to recognize how good he was before he saw it for himself. He was well-rounded, he could climb, he could time-trial, and he could handle himself in the peloton, didn't get scared with the high-speed pushing and shoving. Mainly, he wouldn't quit; he was a stubborn bastard.

With so many different languages on the team, we ended up speaking a kind of pidgin or shorthand with each other. We swapped phrases and colloquialisms, and developed our own jokes. I taught

Chechu to "raise the roof." He was so studious that it was doubly funny when he would act silly, and it sent us all into fits when he raised the roof.

"Chechu, where is the roof?" we'd ask.

The surest way to crack up the boys at dinner or on the team bus was to teach some Americanism to a civilized man like Eki or Pavel. They spoke excellent English, but they puzzled over our more casual terms.

Eki would say to Hincapie, "George, what is that thing you always say, 'How you doing?' "

Pavel was one of the quieter riders, who just did his job and rarely spoke up. We almost never heard from him on the team radios, until finally one day as we were riding, he asked for a mechanic because something was wrong with his bike. Johan dispatched a staffer to fix the problem, and then we heard Johan say, "Okay, Pavel, is it better now?"

"Less or more," Pavel said.

We all cracked up. I tried to explain it to him. "It's '*more* or *less*,' " I said. "The term is 'more or less.' "

"Well, it's the same thing."

"No. No it's not."

"How can it be different?" he said. "Less or more, more or less? What is that?"

He argued with me for the longest time.

We traded harmless insults, based on each other's nationalities, limitations, personalities, and habits. Mostly we shared jokes that nobody else would think were funny.

Every day, I'd go to the gym to work out with George, and we'd sit side by side on the stationary bikes.

One afternoon, George said, "Got any tape?"

"Why?"

" 'Cause I'm ripped," he said, and made a muscle.

Laughter took away the suffering of training. Our jokes were profane and boyish and silly, but within the team, among nine people who knew and loved and trusted each other, mouthing off was an important part of every day, our ritual morale-builder.

"Give me a frickin' tricycle, and I'll kick some ass," I'd say.

We would make up jingles on the bike. Floyd would ride along beside me, and he would start to sing, "Somebody's going to be my bitch today, bitch today, bitch today." All the guys would start screaming, "Aaaaaaaaaaaaaa!!" and get excited.

George had a saying, when he was feeling really good: "No chain." The chain on the bike cranked the wheels and created the tension in your legs that drove the bike forward. But imagine if you didn't have a chain. You'd spin nothing, air, which would feel real easy. So George and I had this thing.

"Man, can you check something for me?" he'd say.

"What?"

"I don't feel a chain," he'd say. "Is there a chain on my bike?"

It became shorthand, "No chain."

I'd say, "Hey, how good do you feel today, George?"

"No chain, no chain."

At the start line of the 2002 Tour de France, I decided to wear a plain, regular workaday blue jersey, indistinguishable from those of my teammates. I wanted to set the tone for the entire race: it was traditional for the defending champion to begin the race in the yellow jersey, but I didn't want to single myself out, and we hadn't done anything to deserve the jersey yet in this year's race. I said to Johan, "Let's earn it."

The prologue would be a seven-kilometer sprint through the majestic streets of Luxembourg, with spires looming as a backdrop, and it was important to me to earn the yellow jersey on that very first day. I'd lost a couple of time trials in tune-up races, and there were the inevitable murmurs in the peloton that maybe I was slipping; every rider would be watching for signs that I was beatable. I wanted to promptly disabuse them of the notion. A win in the prologue would send a message that said, "Hey guys, I'm here, this is the Tour, not some tune-up, and things are different."

There was history at stake, too: I was trying to become only the fourth rider ever to win four straight Tours. The list of others who had done so was short and illustrious: Jacques Anquetil, Eddy Merckx, Miguel Indurain.

But it would be difficult: 189 other riders would try to beat me to the finish, and then there was that timeless opponent, the course itself. It would cover 2,034 miles, and three days before the finish into Paris, we'd still be in the mountains. What that meant was that if you had a bad day, you could run out of road before you could make up the time.

The Tour organizers had made a significant alteration to the route: it would be shorter, but more severe. It was clear that they wanted to design a race that would be more difficult for me, specifically. I'd ridden so strongly and taken such big leaps in the mountains during the previous Tour victories that there was a feeling the race had been boring in the later stages. This time, the course was set up to keep the outcome in doubt until the end, with four key mountain stages in the final eight. Three days before we rode into Paris, we'd still be in the mountains.

In the end, the winner would be the one with the best team, who had managed to stay fresh. I was convinced that Postal was the strongest and best team, especially when we surveyed a field of riders that didn't include Jan Ullrich. He'd had a tough year, injuring his knee, and then wrecking a car after a night out, and he was absent.

On the day of the prologue, Kik went to the cathedral to light the usual candles for good luck, and then she brought the children to the course to see me before the race began. As she moved through the crowds, she wound up on the wrong side of the course, with bikes and follow-cars whizzing by. She had to ask some police officers to help her over the barricade and across the avenue. She carried Luke, while some helpful onlookers in the crowd hoisted the stroller with the girls in it in the air, as if they were crowd-surfing at a concert. When they finally made it across, the crowd cheered.

I sat on a stationary bike, warming up my legs, while Luke drank my Gatorade and examined all the wheels and bike parts with the team mechanics. The twins sat in the stroller facing me, staring up at me, while Kik shoveled baby food into their mouths.

It was time to go. I kissed everybody, and I mounted my bike and headed to the start ramp. Then, after all the other riders had started at one-minute intervals, I flew down the ramp and onto the course. It was a tight, technical course that required a precise ride, and Johan kept up a stream of instructions and chatter in my ear. I kept my eyes on the road in front and ignored the alleys of spectators beating on the barricades. "Very good, Lance, very good, very good," Johan said, and read off my split times.

Johan informed me that the leader was Laurent Jalabert of France, a huge crowd favorite who had announced he would retire after the Tour. I barreled down the last straightaway, chasing the time that "Jaja" had just ridden. I got it—and the stage win—by two seconds. As I crossed the finish line, Kik and Luke shrieked, "Go, yo-yo Daddy!"

The yellow jersey was ours. I knew we would give it right back—it's impossible to defend the jersey from start to finish. It would be smarter to yield it for a few days and conserve energy, and then re-claim it on the way to Paris. Still, it was reassuring to hold it for a day. "It's just good to know I've got it back," I told Bill Stapleton.

After the prologue, I returned to the team hotel and visited with my family. It would be the last relaxed time we'd have together for three weeks. I held the girls, one in each arm, and kissed them, and once again, I schooled my son in who would win the Tour de France.

"What does Daddy do?" I asked.

"Daddy makes 'em suffer in the mountains," he said.

But first we had to get there.

The days were as long as the blacktop in front of you. We rode through the flat champagne country of Reims, and Epernay, a high-speed chase through northern France. We kept ourselves alert and entertained by cranking ZZ Top on the team bus every morning.

ZZ Top was one of Floyd Landis's contributions to the team, and it was an indelible one. Floyd was a loud, rampantly funny pres-ence on the bus, and it was a source of daily entertainment to watch him try to explain ZZ Top to Heras or Rubiera or Eki, jumping around to the lacerating guitar-rock of songs like "She Wore a Pearl Necklace." Finally, Heras—quiet, gentlemanly Roberto—tried to put his foot down. "No more ZZ Top," he pleaded. "No more."

But like it or not, ZZ Top had become our ritual, and so had our morning gathering on the bus. First we'd discuss the strategy and receive our riding orders from Johan, and then the meeting would degenerate and we'd start fooling around. We realized that the bus windows were tinted so darkly that no one could see in, and we'd point out and roar with laughter at autograph peddlers, ticket scalpers, and the loonies in costumes.

Sometimes my friend Robin Williams would climb on the bus and do comedy routines for us. He would imitate a pissed-off Frenchman, smoking Gitanes and drinking Pernod, or he would turn on me and make the guys howl by calling me "The Uniballer," or "The Big Zipper."

One morning when the material had gotten particularly raucous, we decided we should test the privacy of the windows, just in case. We made Johan go outside and look through the windows— and we all mooned him. He never knew it.

It was immature, but it was our way of breaking the tension and the boredom of the flat stages. We wanted to avoid mishaps until we reached the mountains, but these were dangerous sprint stages, windy, with a lot of attacks from out of the pack and always the threat of crashes. The team was riding strongly, but it was wearing on us, especially on Floyd, who we used hard. Floyd had gained such a hotshot reputation from his finish in the Dauphiné that the field was aware of him. We'd make Floyd sprint out hard, and the peloton would go after him, chasing him down and wearing itself out.

Floyd didn't complain. He listened, and he rode hard, and he soaked up knowledge from the veteran riders, and he wouldn't quit. But he had one weakness—his youth. The Tour isn't a young man's event, and in fact it's most punishing on rookies who aren't yet fully hardened and conditioned for a three-week race.

Floyd was nervous. He wasn't sleeping well, and his heart was racing at night. He was worried that he wasn't ready, that he was a liability. One morning we were on the bus together, just the two of us, and we talked. He stared at me, wide-eyed and goateed. "Look," I said, "I need you."

"I know, I know, I know," he chattered.

"Quit it," I said. "Quit fucking freaking out. You're fine. Quit worrying about the team. We're fine."

"But Lance, man, my heart is racing . . ."

"Don't give me any of that," I said. "You're afraid. What are you worried about? Your contract with the team?"

"No."

"I think you are. You need to quit thinking about that. Here's what you need to think about: remember why you're here."

"Okay. Okay."

"No bullshit," I said. "I don't want any excuses. Now you deliver, okay?"

But Floyd wasn't the only tense or tired rider. We all were. We lost track of what day it was, we didn't even know which stage we were riding. Some mornings you woke up feeling like you'd been run over by a truck. But you got back on the bike, and after an hour you felt better. If you were race-hardened, eventually you got in a zone. You reached a point where you had no other concern in life, it consumed everything. You didn't even have the spare energy for a phone call. It was a netherworld state in which we just cycled, and then we'd go lie down until it was time to get up and deal with it again.

In addition to the wind, and the pushing and shoving in the crowded peloton, we were nagged by small mechanical problems. A couple of our guys had to go back to the car for repairs, and it made us jumpy.

One morning I decided to try to ease the strain for all of us. I got on the radio and said, "Johan, I need to come back to the car."

Johan said, "What do you need?"

"I got a problem. I need you to look at my bike."

There was a pause, and I could feel Johan worrying on the other end of the radio. It would take some reorganizing of the team to get me back to the car.

"Johan, you hear me?"

Johan started snapping out instructions. He said, "Okay. Floyd, Chechu, Eki, and Pavel, you go with Lance. He's coming back to the car. We've got to bring him back."

I said, "No, no, I don't need all that. I just need confirmation of something."

"What?"

"I need to know if there's a chain on this bike. Because I can't feel it."

There was another pause, and then Johan's voice crackled on the radio.

"You motherfucker."

Around me, my teammates broke up in laughter.

"I'm serious. Is there a chain back there?"

Stage Four was a team time trial from Epernay to Château-Thierry. It was a test of our ability to ride together as a group, and also a kind of loyalty test, because the time of a team's fifth rider counts for the whole team, which meant that ideally the team should ride together. That was easier said than done, given what could happen at high speeds: flat tires, crashes, or riders falling off the pace. Our time as a team would also be each rider's individual time, so if enough Postal riders rode slowly, it could potentially cost me the overall Tour title.

The ONCE team, led by some superb individual time-trial specialists, was the traditional favorite; no American squad had ever shown much aptitude for team time trials, and in fact it was said to be a Postal weakness. But this time we felt we could challenge the European powers. We went off decked out in our Postal blue skin suits, atop mean-looking black carbon Trek Time Trial bikes. We whirled down the road, averaging around 30 miles per hour, and in some places on the course our speeds rose to around 45. Each guy took a rotation at the front, pulling the others, and when the guy got tired, he faded to the back. There were no mistakes or disasters. Everyone kept up.

We rolled through the finish line together, all nine of us, with a time of 1:20:05—just 16 seconds slower than ONCE, and in second place for the day.

We got through the first week with just one real mishap: about a mile from the end of the seventh stage, Roberto and I got tangled up. We were riding in the middle of the tightly packed peloton, trying to avoid the wild rush to the finish line. Roberto, whose daily assignment was to protect my back, was right behind me. Somebody clipped his wheel, and he fell, and as he went over, his handlebars caught in my rear wheel. My bike locked up—and just stopped.

I hopped off the bike, and yanked on Roberto's handlebars, trying to get them out of my spokes. It took about a minute to get them disentangled, and then I kicked my wheel back into place. Eki pushed me from behind to help me accelerate to the finish. The crash was enough to drop me from third place to eighth. It could have been worse.

But then something worse did happen. Stage Nine was an individual time trial around Lorient, a coastal city with a beautiful boat-studded harbor that had been painted by Impressionists. The time trial was a Tour ritual called "the race of truth," because it was just you against the road and the clock, going flat-out. It was a discipline that rewarded a good technical rider who could make a big solo ride, take a calculated risk without crashing, and I was considered one of the best in the world at it. Since the start of the 1999 Tour, I'd won seven out of nine time trials.

As I warmed up for the stage, I teased one of our mechanics, Jean-Marc Vandenberghe. His father was a road builder, and we had a running joke about it. If I was feeling good, I'd say, "You better call your dad, because I'm going to tear this road up."

The joke was such an old gag between us that by now he didn't even have to ask me how I was feeling. All he had to say was, "Do I need to call my dad?"

That morning I didn't wait for him to ask. I said, "Look, you better call your dad 'cause this road's going to be fucked up when I get done."

But I didn't tear up the road that day. Sometimes you do everything right, and then there are the days when you can't do *anything* right, and this was one. The course didn't especially suit me, and my technique wasn't good. I got off to the wrong cadence, too high, but I couldn't correct it. I knew something was going wrong, but I couldn't quite figure out what.

I lost to Santiago Botero, another great time-trialer who was having a strong season, by 11 seconds. Second place was still a good performance, but because I'd been a heavy favorite, it was treated as a shocking loss and set off a buzz among the peloton: I wasn't quite the Armstrong of the past. Igor González de Galdeano of Spain, who had worn the yellow jersey through the flats, suggested that perhaps my dominance of the race had ended. "The Tour has changed," he announced to the press.

I went back to the hotel in low spirits, and quietly alarmed. If others questioned me, I questioned myself, too. I was also angry at myself for bragging to Jean-Marc that I'd tear up the road.

Standing outside the hotel waiting to see me was a family with a small son who had cancer. The boy's father was a chef from Lyons, the cuisine capital of the world, and they had driven all the way from Lyons to Lorient just to talk to me. They had even brought a French edition of *It's Not About the Bike*. I paused to chat with them on a grassy hillside, and as we spoke, as the sun was setting, the events of the day receded. What they couldn't know was that talking about cancer was like medicine for me.

My encounters with other cancer fighters are often misconstrued: I don't stay involved with cancer just to help others. I do it to help myself. That night, talking with that little boy and his family put me back on my feet. While the rest of the team went to dinner, I stood on the lawn in front of that hotel and kept talking with them, or rather, trying to, as I stammered in my Texas French, and I learned about what the boy had been through. He had spent two five-week stretches in a sterile bubble environment because his immune system had shut down completely—but now he had been cancer-free for a year. It was unimaginable to me what they had been through. *Give me cancer 50 million times more, but don't give it to my kids*, I thought.

I felt peaceful now, just glad to know the boy was well, and that I was, too. I put my arm around him, and left it there. I messed with him, patted his back, and pulled his ears, so I could feel a connection. Finally, I thanked them for coming and went inside to join the team for dinner. But I did so with a surer grasp of what's right and real in the world, and with a sense that there was always a larger community that I belonged to, from which I would always get help in a tough time.

The next day, I kept my mouth firmly shut. I was self-conscious about my bragging before the time trial and determined not to say another word unless I could live up to it. "I'm not going to say anything anymore," I told George. But George said, "Why not? We like to hear that kind of talk."

George made me realize something: the last thing a team needs is self-doubt. Nobody wants to work alongside someone who is unsure of himself, because it's a waste of everyone's efforts. My teammates had put in all those thankless hours on the bike because they believed it was for a winning cause, they had trained with me in the Alps and given up their personal lives because it was a bargain we'd all struck together. That mutual belief gave us momentum, it propelled us down the road and up the mountainsides.

They didn't want to hear, in the middle of the race, that I was suddenly iffy about the job.

By the time we reached the foot of the jagged, rocky Pyrenees, I felt surer of myself again. "We're going to attack, and get the time back," I said.

Stage 11 would take us to a village called La Mongie, halfway up the famed Tourmalet, and I knew what was ahead and exactly how difficult it was. I knew something else, too, which was reassuring: I wouldn't have to do it alone. We were going to come charging up that mountain together, all of us, and when we did, the other riders would drop away. "They'll crack," I promised the team.

The day took us over three monstrous climbs. The first was the Col d'Aubisque, a steep and treacherous 11 miles to over 5,607 feet of altitude. As we approached the Col d'Aubisque, I got on the radio. "Time to ride," I said.

Teamwork on a climb is especially vital: drafting behind a teammate could save me as much as 40 percent of my effort, so that I would be fresh for the final sprint to the finish line. The idea was to use teammates one by one, until they tired. Each served as a kind of booster rocket to get me to the finish line.

Laurent Jalabert sped up the Aubisque in a breakaway that made the roadside fans delirious—but then Postal came down the road chasing him, not far behind. We looked like a huge flying blue wedge, with Ekimov and Hincapie out front.

But as we hit the foot of the climb, Floyd Landis gained a full understanding of why the Tour is the hardest event in the world. His front wheel started the climb—and he just parked. It was like his bike just stopped and decided to go in reverse. He was stunned by the severity of the climb; he simply couldn't keep up with the rest of us. He dropped away. The rider who had swashbuckled through crowds of riders now wove unsteadily up the mountainside by himself, with a stricken look on his face.

We rode on without him. We reached the bottom of the Tourmalet, with George still riding in front. Normally, George wasn't a climber, but we needed him to do some work today, especially with Floyd struggling. The problem was, Tourmalet was one of his most feared climbs, and I knew it.

I said, "George, just pull for the first four or five K, just whatever you can do." George looked at me skeptically. He wasn't sure he could survive it, much less help anybody else. "You can do it, man," I said.

I hung on to his wheel and he pulled until he thought his heart was going to explode. He pulled, and pulled, and began to really suffer. It was an hour-long climb. About 20 minutes into it George was still working at the front, and you could practically see his heart pounding through his open jersey. For once, his mouth hung open and he struggled to breathe. He was just trying to concentrate.

I decided to take his mind off his pain by teasing him a little. I got on the radio, and I said, "Hey, Johan, George just asked me if you could check on when the climb starts."

"This is not the time," George said.

Finally, George dropped away. I started to say something, but I took one look at him, and closed my mouth. He was done—but he'd made an unforgettable effort.

Next, Chechu and Roberto took over—and over the next few minutes they blew the Tour apart. They set such a fast pace that within minutes it crippled most of the field.

We went higher and higher, over roads with no guardrails, and the sun scorched us. There were no more than ten riders who could stay with our pace. The rest had fallen back. We passed Jalabert.

Chechu wore his hat turned backwards to soak up the sweat. I was so hot that I pulled mine off and tossed it into the crowd.

Now Chechu faded, finally spent. Roberto took over. He hammered at the road so hard that he reduced the group to three: himself, me, and the only rider who would be my competition in the coming week, Joseba Beloki of Spain.

I rode just behind Roberto, staring at the back of his curly-haired head as he swayed on his bike. I glanced over my shoulder. The rest of the peloton was strung down the mountain in a scene of pure colorful destruction.

But Roberto's pace was so strong that it even hurt me. Outwardly, I looked fine. I didn't want anyone to see I was in pain, not the directors who might be watching television in their cars, and especially not Beloki, so I tried to stay smooth and settled and straight-faced.

Meanwhile, I said to Roberto just ahead of me, "*Tranquilo, tranquilo*," meaning, "take it easy, take it easy."

Roberto slowed down a little, to my relief. But I did such a good job of hiding my distress that Johan, watching me on a screen from inside the team car, thought I was fine. He saw a chance to open some real time on the field and didn't understand why we had slowed down, so he got on the radio and said, "Roberto, *venga, venga*." "Faster, faster."

So Roberto started to go faster. I said again, "Roberto, *tranquilo*." He slowed down again.

Johan came on the radio again, saying, "*Venga, venga, venga, venga!*"

Finally I got on the radio, and I said, "Goddammit, Johan, tell him to slow down!" Johan relayed the message, and Roberto settled into a pace I could keep more comfortably.

Beloki still doggedly rode on my wheel. I knew he was thinking he could steal the stage win from us. I let him slide between me and Roberto, and for a few minutes we pinned him there.

I could tell from Beloki's face that he was hurting worse than I was. His mouth hung open and his eyes were half-closed.

Suddenly, with about 200 meters to go, I slingshotted past Beloki. I leaped out of my seat and charged hard for the finish line. He couldn't respond.

I took seven seconds from Beloki in the space of less than 50 yards to the finish, and became the leader of the Tour. We had regained the yellow jersey. Everyone else had broken but me, thanks to the team. It was as if they had opened the door, and then stood aside for me, and let me walk through it.

At the finish line I found Johan. "What were you doing?" I said. "I was telling Roberto to slow down and you were telling him to speed up."

He said, "You were hurting?"

"I was fucking *dying*."

"Man, on TV you looked like you weren't even trying."

"No shit?"

At the end of the day, Floyd climbed onto the team bus. He was physically shattered by the severity of the stage. He dropped onto a couch.

"You know, I'm really sorry," he said.

"You had the reverse lights on," I told him.

Someone made a high-pitched sound like a tractor backing up. "Beep, beep, beep, beep!"

The bus erupted into raucous laughter.

We weren't disappointed in Floyd. We'd all been in his shoes before—and while we laughed, we winced for him too, because the first mountain stage in the Tour was a rite of passage for every rider. Floyd had to learn that it was okay to be in pain, to suffer, and to be defeated by a climb.

He was also learning that the Tour would use up every last bit of him; there could be no other concern in his life, except getting back on the bike. It consumed everything. There was no extra energy for any kind of stress. All you hoped to do was fight each specific pain or challenge as it arose, and to hold off the daily exhaustion that made even sitting down an effort.

It was no easy thing to be a rookie in the Tour, but it was particularly grueling to be riding on a team in first place, because it meant riding at the front every day. If Floyd was flattered and surprised to be on our Tour squad in his first year with us, he was scared and self-conscious, too, because he knew we had to choose carefully and take guys who could do the job. He didn't want to hold us back.

I reassured Floyd that he was doing a fine job. His role was to sacrifice himself for the rest of us, and he had done that. Only older, more experienced men could expect to ride strongly in every single stage.

Floyd was amazed. He couldn't believe nine guys, all of us so stressed and tired, could be so forgiving of one another's performances. But that was exactly what made us a strong team. We urged one another on, and teased one another. Sometimes we exceeded expectations, sometimes we fell short, but we always tried to find out if we had more to give. For a rider to discover new capacities he didn't know he had—that was the whole point of the Tour.

Later that night, highlights of the stage came on TV. I ran to

George's room and we watched it together. Here came The Blue Train, as the commentators called us, whirling up the road, with George in front. We both watched in awe how strong our team was. It was a spectacle.

"Man, look at that," I said. "I love the way that looks."

The team wasn't just the riders. It was the mechanics, masseurs, chefs, *soigneurs,* and doctors. But the most important man on the team may have been our chiropractor.

The Tour hurt in a dozen different ways. We were all sore. Sore necks, sore knees, sore hamstrings. Guys got tendinitis all the time. They crashed, or they rode in a fixed position for hours on end, and they got it. They woke up one morning and it was in an elbow or a knee.

They got road rash. Let me explain road rash. It's what happens when you fall off a bike and you skid on asphalt at 40 miles per hour. We're not talking a scraped knee here. We're talking about rolling down the crude rocky asphalt of northern France, and skinning both sides of your entire body, and the front and back, too. It leaves you with scabby, nasty patches where the skin's been scraped off—sometimes to the bone. (A), it hurts; (B), it hurts for days or weeks; (C), you can't sleep. Just rolling over in bed, the mere touch of a sheet could make you wake up and groan in the middle of the night, "*Aaaahh.*" If you crashed and got a bad case of road rash, it could mess you up for the rest of the Tour.

The guy who put us all back together was our chiropractor, Jeff Spencer. Jeff had been with us since my first Tour victory in '99. His contract was just for ten days, but three days into the race, I called a

Postal executive over and said, "Let me tell you something. See that guy over there? That guy's not going anywhere. We need him."

Jeff is part doctor, part guru, part medicine man. He had all kinds of strange gizmos and rituals and cures, a remedy for every condition. He did things we had no explanation for—but they seemed to work. His methods ranged from basic stretching and massage to high-tech lasers, strange wraps, tinctures, and bandages. If you got road rash, he put a silvery wrap on the injury, and shot you with a laser. George swore Jeff's lasers made road rash heal twice as fast.

Sometimes he did things to parts of your body that didn't hurt. Let's say your foot hurt. He'd shoot the laser at your neck, and talk to you about "nerve connections," while you half-listened. But the next day, your foot would be better.

But Jeff had something that was better than any laser, wrap, or electric massager. He had The Tape. It was a special hot-pink athletic tape that came from Japan and seemed to have special powers.

George got a problem with his lower back. Jeff turned him around and started putting hot-pink tape on it. George thought, "How can that help?" But the next day the pain had disappeared— it was *gone*.

We swore by Jeff's pink tape. He would tape the hell out of anything. You had a tweaky knee? He taped it. A guy would start to get tendinitis and he'd say, "Don't worry. No problem. We'll tape it." We all had pink tape on our legs.

Every morning before the stage, he'd tape us all up, different parts of our bodies. He'd do George's back, Chechu's knees. Sometimes we'd be so wrapped up in hot-pink tape that we'd look like dolls, a bunch of broken dolls.

One day, Johan went to him and said, "The tape is too flashy. People see the tape, and they think we're all screwed up."

Jeff said, "What do you want me to do?"

"Tone down the tape," he said. "Can't you get the gray color?"

But the pink tape worked, so we kept it, because it could fix things. It could seriously fix things.

At the end of the day there was a line of riders waiting to see Jeff, because we believed Jeff could fix any and all of our problems. Sometimes guys weren't really hurt, they were just tired, or screwed up mentally, or emotionally. Pena got tired, Pavel got tired, even Roberto got tired. Jeff could fix that, too. While he fixed us physically, he also fixed us mentally. He'd say, "You know, you look a lot better today."

I'd say, "Really?"

"Yeah, I can see it in your face."

If you judged the most important man on the Postal team by the foot traffic in and out of his door, then it was Jeff. Without him, we knew we'd never make it to Paris.

Big Blue kept coming. By now other riders feared us, they dreaded our accelerations, and when they saw us coming, they parted. We'd surge to the front, and they'd say, "Can you please just slow down a little bit?" We'd hear riders from the back of the peloton, yelling, "Please just take it easy, take it easy!" We rode until they slumped over their handlebars, their heads hanging low from their necks like dying tulips.

The idea was not to torture people, but to make them uncomfortable enough that they would have trouble keeping up, much less attacking. We rode as a single entity, the same set to our shoulders and hips, no wasted motion swaying on the bikes, as if we all breathed at the same pace and pedaled at the same cadence.

We won a second mountain stage victory the day after La Mongie, this one to the Plateau de Beille. It was a stage with five vicious ascents, the last to a ski station at the top of a climb that was *hors catégorie*—"beyond category," meaning, you don't want to know. The day was so hard that six riders abandoned the Tour. But I felt great. While other riders felt miserable, I rode behind Big Blue.

We climbed 4,000 feet in ten miles. Again, Chechu and Roberto put everybody out of the race except for me and Beloki—and we still weren't going full-bore. Now we had a chance to stamp our authority all over the race. Roberto sat on Beloki's wheel while I blew by him. I lengthened the lead comfortably and then checked over my shoulder. At the finish I threw up a big two-armed salute, because I knew we had laid the foundation of the overall victory.

For the rest of the race, we just ground our opponents down, putting a little more time on them each day. Stage 14 took us to my old friend Mont Ventoux, which could be seen looming over all of Provence. By the end of the day we'd all but won the overall title, racing up the stony wasteland almost two minutes ahead of Beloki to increase the overall lead to 4:21.

You're supposed to hit the brakes when you're going downhill, but you don't hit the brakes when you're going uphill. That day, we rode so strongly that we were hitting the brakes—uphill. We went so fast into some of the turns that we actually had to slow down.

Afterward, Beloki conceded the race. "I'm going for second," he said. "Today we went to the moon and saw the astronaut."

The last test was a final individual time trial in Mâcon. Sun blazed over a course that undulated through vineyards, alleys of spectators lining the way. I wanted to win it badly—to show that I was still the strongest rider, to make up for the one I had lost early in the Tour. This time I felt good and everything went right, and I did tear up the road.

The rest of the way to Paris, we concentrated on riding safely and luxuriated in our accomplishment. The team was infallible, every man as strong as the next. Pavel rode good tempo in the flats. Roberto and Chechu were awesome on the climbs. Floyd suffered like a dog, but he came through it and added depth. George and Eki were like linebackers, escorting me around like a couple of personal bodyguards, riding in the wind and in crowds.

The race wasn't even over yet, but I said to Bill, "Your first priority is to get every guy back on this team." Chechu was sure to have some other offers, and I knew he was stressing because he loved being on the team as much as we loved having him. I had a talk with him, and assured him we'd pay what it took. He said, "I'm not going anywhere."

Over the years we'd worked to improve the team, staff, and mechanics, and this time it was close to perfect. They'd made life almost easy for me. The most trouble I was in during the whole Tour de France was at La Mongie, on my own teammate's wheel.

Just before the finish in Paris, a young Dutch woman with cancer came to our hotel. Again, it gave me a sense of peace and perspective to talk to a fellow patient. I invited her to come into the dining room with me, and we took a table next to the Postal team and talked for 45 minutes or so. She had a tough story: she had been treated and had relapsed, and been treated again. We talked for a while about her treatment options, and she was curious about the U.S. She asked me, "What did you do?"

"I got treated, I fought like hell, and I got better," I said.

We discussed the treatments in the States, and the merits of American hospitals. She asked me what I ate, and how much I exercised. I told her the truth. "I started out eating a lot of spinach, and then in the end all I could keep down was apple fritters," I said. I told her I'd tried to ride my bike as much as I could, until I fainted one day.

Finally, the conversation drew to a close, and she gave me a present. She had brought clogs, real Dutch clogs, for my whole family. There were five pairs, including tiny ones for the children. I now treasure them as remembrances; she's since passed away.

A few days later, Big Blue rode me into Paris, and I crossed the finish line with an official time of 82 hours, 5 minutes, and 12 seconds and a winning margin of 7:17. I was inexpressibly proud. We hadn't made the slightest tactical error. Not one. We'd grown stronger as the race went on, more secure in our craft, more patient. I felt a sense of achievement I hadn't felt in any of my previous three Tour victories, because of the sheer beauty of that team performance.

Other people seemed to feel it, too. In Paris, for the first time, the headlines seemed warm toward us. The *Le Parisien* headline saluted both Jalabert and me in the same sentence: MERCI JAJA . . . BRAVO ARMSTRONG. I was grateful for the compliment. A French wine dealer was quoted as saying, "A man's value is his spirit, not his country." Also, suddenly the French had a nickname for me: the Boss.

At the finish line, I spoke French to the local press. "I love France," I said. Perhaps people finally understood what I'd been trying to express, whether in French or English, all along: the Postal riders weren't robots, or cold corporate American merchants. Rather, we were on a search for the perfect ride, the most excellent technique, and that was not a matter of coldness, but of love. "This is not theater, it's sport," I said. "I believe in performance and in the beauty of the race."

But more than anything, I believed in my teammates—and I wanted to do something for them. Each year we had a Postal Service victory party for 300 or so people at the Musée d'Orsay, the grand old train station that had been converted to a museum of French painting. It was a luxurious party, but we would be scattered at separate tables. I wanted to do something more personal, so we could have a celebration together, just the nine of us. For weeks they had slaved, dealing with tendinitis and road rash, sleeping cramped and sore in small hotels. For this night I wanted them to feel like rock stars, because to me, that's what they were. I wanted them to feel like every inch the winners.

Kik helped me arrange for a small private-party room at the Hôtel de Crillon, where I always stayed on the last night in Paris, because they flew the Texas flag over the Champs-Elysées (the place earned my lifelong business for that). Five S-class Mercedes picked the guys up and drove them to the hotel. Every other team rode buses to get to their parties, but our guys got picked up by Mercedes.

The cars brought the team and their families to a private reception room at the Crillon, where a banquet was laid out. We all shook hands and I passed each one of them an envelope, and they stuck them in their pockets, to open later.

We sat around with our families, nibbling from a buffet table, drinking and telling stories, and falling out. We laughed about trying to translate ZZ Top lyrics. Kik came down and joined us, and she strolled into the room like a fashion diva in black slacks and a white blouse with a string of pearls. All of the guys burst out singing ZZ Top, "She wore a PEARL NECK-LACE!"

Finally, we split up and the guys left to make the rounds of some Paris nightspots. As they got back into the limousines, some of them opened their envelopes. It was traditional, and only right, for the Tour winner to give the $400,000 prize money to his teammates, and they assumed their checks were in the envelopes. What they didn't know was that I had doubled the amount, as a personal thanks from me. Guys started calling me on my cell phone from their cars, and screaming. In the background, I could hear an envelope tearing, and someone said, "This is a mistake, right? He put in one too many zeroes."

We scattered across Paris and were out till the late hours; I don't know where all of them landed in the end. Some, like George, stayed up all night. Floyd went to bed earlier than anybody. He hadn't seen his wife in two months, so they left at midnight. He was so tired he didn't know how to put it into words. Even taking a shower felt like an effort.

He fell into bed—and he didn't wake up until four P.M. the next day. Even then he was only awake long enough to eat something, and then he went back to sleep *again* until ten the next morning. He wouldn't feel normal for a month afterward.

But he had helped us win, and in doing so, he had helped himself. He paid off all his debts, and he got a new Postal contract: a generous two-year deal that would pay him more than double his salary. "I've never had a two-year contract—at anything," he marveled.

Why engage in a collective effort rather than an individual one, even when you wonder, "What's in it for *me*?"? Self-interest is isolating. When you work in collaboration, you're responsible to each other, and therefore much less likely to shirk your responsibilities or cheat your partner. Teamwork is not only performance-enhancing, it's comforting. You are never alone, and whether you have a six-mile climb up an alp and a cadre of attackers behind you, or a round of chemo in front of you, that's extremely reassuring.

Pro athletes talk all the time about "my game." But your game doesn't belong to you when you're on a team—there's no such thing as "my" game, there is only *the* game. Your effort belongs to your teammates and theirs belongs to you, and they're inextricable. The same is true of any gathering of people in one place, for any purpose.

To me, the definition of a team is a group of people who share the same aim, experience, and values. By that definition, the alliance between people fighting cancer qualifies as my team also. I am always aware of them, just as they are of me, and I still meet people who are frightened and fearful, who constantly remind me that I used to be sick, that I got well, that they are following the story. And unlike a race, the story doesn't end.

You think it's over, but it's not. It's never over.

On the morning after I crossed the finish line in Paris, Bart came to see me at the Hôtel de Crillon. I was in a suite doing interviews and struggling with the sleepiness and a mild hangover when he appeared in the hall outside my room, pale and red-eyed. Bill met him at the door, took one look at him, and said, "What's the matter?"

Bart struggled to speak. He'd gotten a panicked call from Austin that morning: his younger brother, David, had just been diagnosed with a horribly aggressive form of cancer and was in St. David's Hospital, receiving blood transfusions.

I came out to the hall. "What's going on?"

"He just found out his little brother has cancer," Bill said.

I stared at Bart for a second. "Okay," I said. "Let's go to work. Let's fix it."

I put my arm around Bart's shoulders, and Bill put an arm around him, and together we steadied him and got him into the suite. My room was in chaos; we were trying to pack, and the kids were running around, and some press people were there. Bill asked the press to leave.

Slowly, Bart told us the story. His kid brother, David, had stubbed his toe in a game of pickup basketball over the weekend. It had gotten terribly bruised and swollen, but David just thought it was broken. The next day, he got a nosebleed that wouldn't stop. Blood gushed down his face, and finally he had to go to the emergency room, where a staff doctor diagnosed leukemia and admitted him to the hospital in order to start transfusions. Now, virtually overnight, he was in a precarious state and could die.

David Knaggs was 31 years old. His wife, Rhiannon, was pregnant with their first child.

It was the middle of the night back in the States, but I didn't care. I started calling and e-mailing all of the cancer doctors I knew. I called Dr. Jeff Murray, the child-cancer specialist from Fort Worth who had treated Kelly Davidson. I also called Steve Wolff, the chairman of the LAF Scientific Advisory Committee who had consulted on my own case and steered me to the right specialists. I woke Dr. Wolff up, and he immediately offered to consult. He promised to check on David's status, and in the meantime recommended that we quickly get David transferred to a cancer center.

"We've got to get your brother moved," I told Bart.

Bart just nodded, still too devastated to talk much. "Listen,

I'm here with you," I said. "You can't fall apart. We've got to get a move on."

Next, we set up a human chain to help get Bart home to Austin. I reached Jim Ochowicz, who was still in Paris, asked him to meet Bart at the Paris airport and take care of him. Och met him at curbside, got his bags checked in and upgraded him, and held his hand, literally.

Just before Bart boarded the flight, Steve Wolff called back with worrisome news. David's white blood-cell count was 177,000—and the normal white blood-cell count for a young man is between 4,000 and 7,000. "He's got about thirty times too many white blood cells, and that indicates a lot of disease," Dr. Wolff said. "It's very aggressive."

The immediate danger, he said, was leukostasis, a life-threatening thickening of the blood. "He's at a critical juncture," Wolff said. He recommended that David be moved, and quickly, to a specialized facility equipped to deal with aggressive leukemias; otherwise he could deteriorate quickly. "He needs to make some immediate progress against the disease," he told us.

Bart got on his plane, worried sick. He and Och flew to the States with Bart sitting bolt upright. Finally they touched down in Chicago, and as he changed planes for Austin, Bart talked again to Steve Wolff. David was going to be moved by ambulance to the M. D. Anderson cancer facility in Houston, where a specialist was waiting to admit him.

Bart landed in Austin, got in a car, picked up his mother, and began driving to Houston. He was so tired that his mom had to sing songs to keep him awake as he drove. They reached M. D. Anderson at about four A.M., and David's new cancer doctors, Archie Bleyer and William Wierda, met them there. What happened next was a testament to the power of science.

By seven A.M. they had performed a bone biopsy on David and

typed the cancer. Next, they performed a procedure to lower his dangerously high white blood-cell count. They gradually removed the blood from his body, pulling it from his inner thigh, in order to remove some of the white cells. They centrifuged the blood and put it back into his body. By noon, the procedure was complete and his white blood-cell count had fallen below 100,000.

The last time Bart had laid eyes on David, his younger brother was a robustly healthy man with an easy way about him, one of the many smart, athletic young Austinites who'd found a good life in the city, who tapped at a computer by day and played pickup basketball by night, and who was so sure and secure in his future that he was starting a family.

Now Bart stood by David's bedside. In 24 hours, David had acquired small blue bruises all over his body. They were the marks from the capillaries that were bursting and bleeding inside him because he had no platelets. His breathing was labored and shallow, because there was a mass in his chest.

Once David was stabilized, he embarked on a course of clinical-trial chemotherapy, a regimen only available at specialized cancer centers. By August 1, he was undergoing the rigors and toxins of chemo, and he had a fighting chance to survive.

I talked to Bart every day, and I sent David handwritten notes regularly. "I believe in you," I wrote. "I know that what you're doing is even harder than what I did. I see how hard it is on your brother. But I know you're strong, and he's strong. I'm just another guy who's had cancer, and who knows that you can do this."

David did well until November, when his health went sideways. He lost the use of his hands and feet, the result of nerve damage. He could move one finger. That was it. The doctors began talking about a bone-marrow transplant and looking for a donor, testing the members of his family for a match.

David's wife, Rhiannon, spent most of her pregnancy sleeping on a Murphy bed in his room at M. D. Anderson. One evening, as David slept, she went into labor. Rather than wake him, she rushed with her mother to the Texas Women's Hospital. Later, as she fought through her contractions, she reached David by phone. She lay there in the delivery room, while David talked to her soothingly. David listened on the other end of the receiver as his first child came into the world. Isabella Knaggs was born on November 24, 2002.

At Christmas, they found a perfect sibling match for David's bone-marrow transplant: Bart.

On the day after Christmas, my 36-year-old best friend went to Houston to begin the process for harvesting his bone marrow, so it could be transplanted into his brother. After a series of EKGs and MRIs, to make sure he was perfectly healthy, the doctors put Bart on Neupogen, the blood-boosting drug that I'd been given during my own chemo. They also gave him a series of shots in order to build up his stem cells. Twice a day for five straight days, Bart had to get shots in his stomach from a long hypodermic needle.

The shots and the drugs gave him terrible bone aches. He complained of horrible, dull, incessant pains. I knew exactly what he was talking about: they're called bone flares, and chemo patients get them all the time. One minute you're lying in bed, feeling okay, and the next minute a deep pain flares through the center of your bones, deep down below your muscles, where it seems no painkiller could ever reach.

I teased Bart, trying to keep things light, but it hurt me to know that my best friend finally, fully understood the cancer experience. "Oh-ho," I said. "Now you've joined the bone-pain fraternity."

On New Year's Eve, they siphoned Bart's blood out of him, and centrifuged it, taking it from his left arm and putting it back into his right arm. They separated out the plasma. It was difficult to grasp that what was left, a small yellow drip bag with some fluid in it, contained stem cells from Bart's bones and was his brother's best chance to live. The transplant was done: some of Bart's life passed into David.

It took 100 days before we knew whether the transplant was successful. Each day went by, and Bart hoped, and I watched from afar, sending messages from my various travels. "The strength is in *you*," I wrote to David. "You've just got to believe it."

One day in early May, Bart called me. His voice trembled as he said, "David is well, and he's coming home."

On May 6, 2003, David came home to Austin. He was temporarily leukemia-free, and his platelet count was normal. He was still on medications for nerve pain, and he was 50 pounds lighter—cancer takes the mass out of you. He'd lost his job, and the body he knew, and he had a lot of rehab ahead, with an uncertain outcome. But he was home.

I wasn't there when he came home, because I was in Europe, but I sent him a present. It was a bike, a black Trek mountain bike, and a fine-looking thing. Bart mounted it on rollers and plugged it into a windtrainer in David's living room. David rode it every day, as part of his rehab. He sat and watched Cubs games and rode his bike. We hoped his strength would return, but it didn't. A month later he relapsed and as of this writing he was back with his team of doctors at M. D. Anderson, starting the fight all over again.

We don't do anything alone, none of us. I certainly didn't fight cancer alone, or regain my health through some extraordinary solo effort. I survived with the help of six different doctors, four chemo cycles, three surgeons, a devoted mother, dozens of tirelessly caring friends, and several much-cussed-at nurses, including my oncology nurse LaTrice Haney. An important fact was that they didn't disagree or fight amongst themselves. My friends took turns caring for me, and none of my physicians objected to a second opinion or declined a consultation. Instead, they worked together to heal me. We could only try to do the same for David.

When I first won the Tour in 1999, I knew my old cancer ward was following my progress. Each day I thought about my old hallway at the Indiana University Medical Center in Indianapolis, where I suspected that LaTrice turned on the TV and watched, nervously, to see if my lung capacity would hold up in the mountains. I knew that each morning, LaTrice came to work and pointed to the TV and proudly said to whoever she was treating, "He was a patient here." I still know it.

Each time I cross that finish line, she jumps around the room, hugging nurses and doctors and patients. Once she said, "You felt us. I know you felt us." And I did.

Who would want to be a singleton, when you could have all that? Anyone who imagines they can work alone winds up surrounded by nothing but rivals, without companions. The fact is, no one ascends alone.

CHAPTER 7

My Park Bench

I'll be honest with you: I don't wake up every morning thinking *I want to be an inspiration to somebody today.* Some days I don't even want to put shoes on. I just want to wander around barefoot, dragging the cuffs of my jeans in the Texas grass, and think about nothing more complicated than whether to drink a beer or play golf, or both. Usually, I decide to drink a beer for every hole of golf I *would* have played.

For a while, after I won the Tour for the fourth time, I quit shaving. I'd get up in the morning and look in the mirror, and think, *Well, why should I? Who cares?* The stubble on my chin grew until it was patchy and uneven, and my friends called me "Chewbacca," or "Grizzly Adams."

College said, "What are you doing that for?"

I was doing it because beer and a beard were my puny versions of excess.

"It's all I have," I said.

But eventually, I got tired of it. Hard as I try, slacking doesn't agree with me. Everybody needs something to do with their days, to occupy their mind and energies, and in my case that's especially so. I don't just need to take my edge off; I need to wear it off, saw it off, and sand it off. When I've let myself go for too long, gotten way down in the slackage, I look at myself in the mirror, unhappily, and say, "You sorry sack of slack." And I get back on my bike.

But I can't ride in the Tour de France forever, and eventually, I'll have to find something else to do. I guess my next career won't be in diplomacy. Here's something else to consider about retirement too: if the Joux-Plane was my hardest day on a bike, it was still easier than giving a speech.

One day, like it or not, I'll be faced with the inevitable cooling of my career—and then what? What will I do when my muscles and tendons don't respond to the bidding from my brain, and I'm vulnerable to upset, and the stage victories don't come in the thick clusters they used to? Or when I suffer a bad-luck crash I can't recover from? These are all things that could determine when I quit.

My plan is to keep racing through 2004 and beyond, and to try to win a record-tying fifth title. Whether I can actually do it is another matter: people constantly ask me about the record, but I'm superstitious, and I know too much about the race, the accidents that can happen and the way a body can give out, to say that I'll do it.

The greats will tell you that a fifth Tour was hard, and a sixth was impossible. In 100 years, no one has ever won six, and the very best have tried. It's as if there's an invisible barrier. Indurain won five straight from 1991 to '95 and made a valiant attempt at a sixth in '96, but on a big climb to Les Arcs in the seventh stage, his body failed him. Instead, Denmark's Bjarne Riis won the tour. Jacques Anquetil won his fifth in 1964 but then vanished from the podium entirely. The great Eddy Merckx was going for a sixth in 1975 when he was dealt a vicious blow by an irate fanatic: a man leaped from the crowd and punched him in the stomach as hard as he could. Two days later he was still sore and laboring, and he was finally beaten on a mountainside by Bernard Thévenet.

Bernard Hinault had a catastrophic crash en route to his fifth title in 1985, when he was knocked down by another rider during a sprint stage. He crossed the finish line bleeding from his nose, and went on to barely win over teammate Greg LeMond. The next year, it was LeMond who prevented him from winning his sixth.

You just have to accept that some day you're going to fail or fall off your bike. The one thing you can't prepare for in the Tour is a crash. So be it. I'll just lie there, and then get up and go to the beach, and say, "I'm okay. Bring me some sunscreen, and some margaritas."

There is always the possibility that my career could end as the result of a crash, or some kind of injury, or a freak accident. I suppose there is the remote but scary chance that a hostile crazy on the roadside could decide to attack, as Eddy Merckx learned. It's one of the charms of the Tour that it's an open-air event with free admission. You don't need to go through a turnstile to watch the race; you can just wait by the side of the road and it will pass by. The crowd has always been a presence and sometimes an active part of the race; spectators push riders up the hills, clap them on the back, applaud them, hand them food and drinks. It's part of the atmosphere that fans leap out and scream, whether they are irate, or silly, or over-served. I ignore them, because it happens hundreds of times each Tour. I try not to think about whether someone could come for me with something more than an angry expression.

Once in a mountain time trial in Chamrousse, all of a sudden some guy came out of nowhere and started chasing me, holding a magazine and a pen. He said, "Can I have an autograph, can I have an autograph?"

I looked over at him and said, sarcastically, "I'll tell you what. Just let me finish what I'm doing here, and I'll come back and get you later."

George heard that story that night and he fell out laughing. "I can't believe you said you'd come back and get him later," he said.

I prefer to believe in the basic benevolence of fans. I'm more concerned about the possibility of a crash. All cyclists were reminded of just how dangerous the sport can be when Andreï Kivilev was killed. Andreï died in the early spring of 2003 after suffering a fractured skull in a crash in Stage 2 of the annual Paris-Nice race. He was a wonderful, attacking rider who always rode at the front when a mountain loomed. I loved to race with him because when he was in the race, and when the road went uphill, you knew he would lay it all out. Man, was he an attacker. And the best in him seemed to come out in the toughest races, as his fourth-place finish in the 2001 Tour had shown us.

Andreï left behind a wife and a six-month-old baby. I will remember him, always, as a gentleman, a friend, and a competitor who brought forth the best qualities in his opponents.

I hope to finish my career healthy and whole, and to be intelligent enough and self-aware enough to walk away when it's my time to stop. I might even stop a lot sooner than people expect—maybe one morning I'll just wake up and decide not to do anything more strenuous than coaching my kids in T-ball.

I don't want to stretch out my career if it means going out on my face, which is not a pleasant thought. I don't want to linger on too long, until I'm hanging on at the back of the peloton. That's not for me; I can't ride the race in the back. When you're not at the front, but just hanging on, that's when it hurts most of all, down deep where muscle meets bone, and it's a different, more hopeless kind of pain. The leader of the race feels pain, but because he has a good chance of winning, it doesn't feel so bad. When you're at the back, there's not much recompense for the hurting. There's just the honor of finishing.

I often wonder what I would do if somebody put a big chunk of time into me, passed me on a mountainside the way I've done to other riders. The first chance they get to stick it to me, oh, man. I want to get out before that happens. Hopefully I'll know it, and the people around me will know it, and I'll just go ahead and quit.

I'm not obsessed with winning a fixed number of Tours, because the only record that ever mattered to me is this: there had never been even one Tour victory by a cancer survivor. After the physical, mental, and emotional rigors of chemo, if I'd lost even 2 percent of my capacities, I'd be noncompetitive. I don't think anyone, including myself, expected such a spectacular recovery. What I didn't reckon on was that cancer would provide such a focus, a reprioritization. Winning the Tour became my way of saying to cancer, "You haven't beaten me, and you can't beat me."

The determining factor in the length of my career won't be a record. My career will play out year to year, and what will keep me in the saddle is not a number, but happiness. The way I ride has always been based on a simple fact: I love riding my bike. It's just too hard to do it otherwise. How long will I continue to love it at the world-class level? That needs to be checked regularly. I can't answer that or guarantee it.

In sport you're always on record for what you've done, for what you've said, the way you've acted. Everything is measured, either by a clock or by a camera. It's all on record, or on video; the data is there for all to see. But there is no measurement that can tell me how happy I am, on or off the bike. All I know is that for every minute that I improve physically, there are days when I may become 45 seconds less motivated, as I understand more about what achievement can and cannot do for me as a person, and what it costs.

So it's not my job to speculate on what my place in cycling history will be, and whether I'm remembered or forgotten, because—not to be disrespectful about it—who holds the record for most Tour victories won't be my problem in ten years.

I just hope I'll be content when I stop. Why should what you do between the ages of 20 and 30 be the apex of an entire life? In Texas you see it all the time: people who are still dining out on their finest moment on a high school state championship team. But the athlete is just one segment of a person; in my case there are also the cancer advocate and a father who takes his children to preschool.

I think one of the real traps of being a prominent athlete is that you get used to a big spike in adrenaline and attention, and that can cause a lot of problems later. You wake up one morning and find you need a big jolt. But not much surprises me anymore about celebrity, and the main thing I know about it is that it's not good for you. When I'm done cycling, I'll disappear. I've got no contract that says I have to appear on TV screens and talk to the press. I look forward to thinking more, and to listening more. I don't have much interest in interviews and speaking engagements; they are, to me, complicated affairs, and life is too short to be complicated.

One reason I love Girona is that on the street where I live, I'm just another neighbor. There's a small café that I can see from my window, with deep wicker chairs on the sidewalk, and I love to sink into one and drink coffee and read the paper.

What I'd like to do when I'm retired is take the kids to Europe for three months, and live in Girona and go to all the races, as a spectator, so that I can show them how beautiful the world is from a bike. I'd like to show them why Spain is a paradise. In Spain, you learn about design as revelation: plazas lead to inner plazas, walls within walls open into surprising spaces, where hidden fountains run and ferns hang from the ancient brick. Streets cascade down to broader plazas and *ramblas*, overlooking crescent beaches and ports choked with the masts of sailing yachts, and you can hear the chimes from the ropes of the rigging.

On a bicycle, you never know what's around the next bend, when a view may open up, or the Alps may shear off to the sea. Even when I'm 50, I'll probably still be riding in all weather. I'll put on every piece of clothing I own and ride for the pleasure of the bike, sightseeing.

A bicycle is the long-sought means of transportation for all of us who have runaway hearts. Our first bike is a matter of curb-jumping, puddle-splashing liberation; it's freedom from supervision, from carpools and curfews. It's a merciful release from reliance on parents, one's own way to the movies or a friend's house. More plainly, it's the first chance we have to choose our own direction.

It's the first wheeled machine we ever steer solely by ourselves, and perhaps for that reason we have intense affection, and strangely specific memories, of the bikes we've owned. I myself have had hundreds of them by now, but they stay with me, like old friends. The physical familiarity you gain with a bike is something you don't feel for any other vehicle, no matter how sweet the ride. There are times when I swear a bike is merely an extension of my arms and legs. All these years later, I still have a faint sensation of my first bike, a Schwinn, how the rubber handgrips molded to my palms, and how the soles of my sneakers grabbed the teeth of the pedals.

Even in the midst of a hard day on a bike, beneath every pain and stress is the sense of relief and pleasure that I'm able to ride again. I ride to prove that in a scientific and highly mechanized era, the human body is still a marvel. In cycling there is no outer skin of metal to protect you from the elements. You have only your flimsy clothing, and this makes it a sport that is as sensuous as it is severe. The cyclist experiences great beauty, sublime views, and the swooping exhilaration of a mountain descent, but there's a penalty on the body for cycling, too, a physical toll in exchange for the beauty of the trip that reminds riders that they're human.

A bicycle, no matter how elaborate the technology or how advanced the composite that it's made of, remains driven by the body. There is something fundamental about a bike: a frame with a crank, a chain and two wheels, powered by nothing more than my own legs. On a bike, you are under your own power, directed by your own hand. Your motor is yourself.

For now, I still crave the race. I understand that we're only given a couple of shots, and that this may be my only chance to win it . . . again.

An athlete has to somehow figure out how to enrich the people around him, and not just himself. Otherwise he's purposeless.

I'm still sorting out what I can and can't do for other people. I can be a good-luck charm, a hopeful example, a companion in suffering, an advisor, and a good listener. I can try to win the Tour de France over and over again, and in doing so, pound cancer into the ground. I can tell people the one thing I know for sure about the disease, which is that they aren't alone: the illness is so big, so widespread, and so common, that it affects nearly everybody—friends, family, people in the workplace or at your school. Mainly, I can just try to be helpful.

But sometimes, I'm not so helpful. There are occasions when I simply don't know what to say to someone experiencing the ravages of the disease. In September of 2002, I went to the White House to promote cancer research and make a plea for more resources and funding. Before the presentation, someone in the White House press office arranged for me to meet privately with a Hodgkin's Disease patient named Paul de la Garza, a journalist from the *St. Petersburg Times* who was undergoing chemo. After he was diagnosed, a friend had given him a copy of *It's Not About the Bike*, and he had followed the Tour. When he heard that I would be visiting the White House to promote cancer research, he arranged for a meeting through a contact. He wrote later of our meeting: "Who better, I thought, to give me a moral boost or a morale boost than the world's most remarkable cancer survivor?"

But I'm not remarkable; I'm like anybody else, and if you catch me at the wrong time I'm not good for much. As I was introduced to de la Garza, we were ushered into a small anteroom near the Blue Room to talk, but the White House was on a very strict schedule and the protocol was very clear. There wasn't a lot of time, and I was nervous over the prospect of meeting with the president. I tried to listen as I was given some things to sign, posters and magazines.

De la Garza began to ask me some very specific questions about his cancer, what to do, what not to do. I fumbled for replies. I didn't have the $64,000 answer for every cancer question, but I gave him my standard one, which I believe to my core: find the best doctors you can, and trust the hell out of them.

"How do I survive this?" he asked.

I answered, honestly, "Listen to your doctors. Get the very best treatment."

But that advice, as he put it later in an article he wrote about the experience, was "not exactly an epiphany."

His left arm was hurting, his veins were burning, and other parts of his body were rebelling against the treatment. But the main part of him that was rebelling was his mind. He had seven chemo treatments left, and he was getting weaker with each one. I knew exactly what he was experiencing—the nausea, and the taste of tin in the roof of his mouth. I could still smell the stuff myself. He was demoralized, and he had come to meet me hoping for something more.

"How do I survive when I can't stand the thought of another IV in my arm?" he asked.

"The misery is part of getting better," I said. "You have to welcome it."

What I meant was this: misery is the cure. You must embrace it, because it's what may save you. You can alter any experience with your mind—it's up to you to determine what the quality of each moment is. Concentration and belief can make even chemo, no matter how sickening it is, a positive experience. It takes practice, but it's possible. I used to tell myself, when I threw up or when it burned so badly to urinate, that the sensations represented the cancer leaving my body. I was pissing it out, puking it out, coughing it out. I wasn't going to dwell on whether I was going to die. There were those in medicine and those outside it who thought I *would* die—but I chose to be around doctors and nurses who believed I could make it.

I had help from LaTrice Haney, my oncology nurse. Once, deep in the misery of chemo, I asked LaTrice if I would ever get out of the hospital. LaTrice said, "Lance, each time you walk in here, you will walk out again. And there will be a time when you don't come here anymore at all—because you'll be cured."

I should have told all of these things to Paul de la Garza. Or maybe I'd have been better off just sympathizing with his plight and telling him this simple, stark truth: yeah, cancer was the best thing that ever happened to me—but I don't want to do it again.

Instead, all I said was, "When the treatment is over, you bounce back quick. At least, I did."

Then a White House staffer interrupted us and I was ushered into the Blue Room for my brief address with the president. De la Garza was left in the anteroom, clearly disappointed in our meeting.

"That was it," he wrote;

Our meeting lasted maybe five minutes. While I appreciated his time—I later learned it was his 31st birthday—and relished the trappings of the White House, he really didn't say anything that knocked my socks off, the sort of nugget I was fishing for to get me through the tunnel. Still, the meeting helped, because it made me realize something else. On the drive home from work the night before, I actually had tears in my eyes in anticipation of our meeting. I was counting on him for some revelation to make everything better. Because of his story I was treating him as if he held the secret for my cancer cure. But what I discovered almost immediately, before I walked out the gates of the White House even, is that I don't have to turn to the rich and famous, to the heroes of the sports world, to get me through the anxiety, the depression, and the fear of the what-ifs. My heroes are right in front of me, ordinary folks who every day make my life better. At the top of the list I include my wife, my kids . . . my family, my friends, my co-workers, my nurses, my doctors.

He was right; heroism is impossible to fulfill—the bar is too high. If some people want a revelatory experience, I can't answer the request. More often than not, a hero is a person who acts without thinking, anyway. If ten people, or a million people, want to say that you're a hero, the only thing you can do is say thank you, just keep going about your day, and understand that *trying* to be a hero is not the most useful purpose you can serve.

The most useful purpose I can serve is to tell people who are suffering that it's an absolutely important human experience to be ill, that it can change how you live, and that it can change other lives, too.

Sometimes I'm successful in imparting the message, and sometimes I'm not. I wasn't so successful with de la Garza. But not long after, I met a woman who was ill and had lost her hair. The only people who had ever seen her with her wig off were her doctors, but when I visited her, she took it off. We had our picture taken together. I will never get tired of befriending people with cancer, and I'll always say, "Come on over here, get right up next to me."

It's not a burden, it's an opportunity, and I'll do it until they ask me not to. Someday there might be a 15-year-old girl who won't know or care who I am, and someone else can step in and be her in-spiration. Until then, I'll try to meet every request, every person who can use some help.

I'd like to learn to use my influence to shape thinking about can-cer on a larger level, too. Maybe I can even help shape opinions, pol-icy, and the flow of money on cancer. After I visited the White House that day, I continued on to Capitol Hill, with the same mission, to promote cancer research and ask for more funding. I met with, in or-der, Senator Ted Kennedy (D-Massachusetts), Senator Sam Brown-back, a conservative from Kansas, and Senator Diane Feinstein (D-California). The meetings perfectly illustrated the commonality we all have on the subject of cancer.

Senator Kennedy's son, Teddy Jr., lost a leg to bone cancer when he was a boy. The senator ushered us into his office and began show-ing me the pictures on his wall, of brothers and sisters gone. He talked a little about each of the people in the pictures, and then he turned to another picture, of his son.

"When my son had cancer, I tried everything I knew to distract him," the senator said. "But the only thing that would keep his mind off of his cancer was the Celtics-Lakers series. So I got tickets to every game I could, and we would go, and for a couple of hours he wouldn't think about it."

He showed me another picture: Ted Jr. on a ski slope wearing a prosthetic, and raising his arms, triumphant. He had just won a gold medal at the Paralympics. As I turned to speak to the senator, I real-ized that tears were streaming down his face.

The next office we went to was that of Senator Brownback. I knew of the senator because he had survived a bout with cancer, like me. The senator was very certain that the cancer had altered his view of both life and the afterlife: he had become a born-again Christian. We settled onto a sofa.

"Tell me how cancer has changed your spirituality," he said.

There it was again, that uneasy question. I wondered how to explain to the senator that my spirituality is mine, and mine alone. But before I opened my mouth, my friend Jeff Garvey, the chair of my cancer foundation, understood my dilemma and jumped in. "Lance's wife, Kristin, is Catholic," he said quickly. "And he has a chapel in his house."

I was grateful for the out, but I decided to be straight. I gave him my honest answer, and said, "I relied on my doctors, and the medicine and the science, they were my hope." I added that I believed in my personal responsibility in my cure, to educate myself, and to combat the disease.

The senator is a spirited and vigorous cancer fighter, and he said, "We need to set a date, and say that within the next ten years we want to have a cure." It was my kind of fighting speech, very determined. But we both knew the reality, too, which is that cancer is not just one disease but 250 diseases, each with separate symptoms and treatments and potential cures. So we're not talking about one cure, but 250. We parted with a handshake and an agreement to see each other again.

My final stop was to see Senator Feinstein, for what was the most lighthearted of our interviews. She was a charming lady without an ounce of pretense. We gathered in her office and sat down and talked for a while about the importance of funding for more cancer research, and of better information, too.

Then she said, "Let me ask you something."

"Sure," I said.

"I ride my bike, too. Does your butt hurt?"

I threw back my head and shouted with laughter. "Yep," I said. "That's why my shorts are padded."

By the time I left Washington, I had new questions about my peculiar status as an athlete. Athletes are public figures, yet we tend to believe we shouldn't engage in politics or the issues of the day because our job is just to be excellent with our bodies. But to me, that's not quite enough. It's not about the bike. It never has been. It's about causes: I think everybody should have one.

I still struggle with whether or not it's my responsibility to make public statements. For instance, as war with Iraq became imminent, both the American and the foreign press wanted to know my thoughts on the subject, since I'm friendly with President George W. Bush. My reply was that I wasn't in favor of war—who is?—but that I support my president, and our troops. Somebody said, "So you disagree with him?" I said, "Well, the nice thing about America is that it's the kind of place where it's okay to disagree with a friend."

But a far more significant answer to the question came from my friend Lee Walker. One afternoon I was sitting around visiting with Lee at his house, and I asked him what he thought about Iraq.

Lee said, "I'll tell you two things. First of all, I'm not sure what I think, but I'm an American and I follow my president, I go where he goes. But the second thing is, that's a global issue and I can't affect it. I can't do a damn thing about Iraq, and Saddam Hussein doesn't know me from Adam. But here's what I *can* do. I can go down to the street corner and make *that* place a better place. I can do that. I can affect the park. I can affect the bus stop. I can go affect that park bench right over there, and maybe change somebody's day, or minute, or life. I can do that."

Lee pointed to a bench on the sidewalk in front of his house. Lee had literally bought the bench and placed it out front, just to contribute something to the neighborhood. His neighborhood is full of elderly people, and they walk to various shops for what they need. It occurred to Lee that they might need a place to sit down and rest their feet. So now that's what you see in front of Lee's house, people sitting on the bench, with bags, resting their feet.

Lee says his philosophy is just to break problems down to their smallest parts, right down to the person or to the child, and work backwards from there. "There's a lot we can't do anything about," Lee explained. "But we can affect the things right here in front of us, make them better, as best we can."

So that's what I'd like to do, too. I'd like to build park benches. Cancer is my park bench. And so are the kids in my arms.

There's no difference between a man with no power and a man with power who doesn't use it at all. That's what I've come to believe about athletes and participating in the issues of the day. If I were religious I'd say cancer advocacy is what God would like me to do, but I'm not. So I'll simply say that's what I have the opportunity to do, and what I'm designed to do.

When a book is over, people always wonder what happened next. Does he live or does he die, does he win or does he lose, is he happy or is he unhappy? Who does he turn out to be?

Here are just a few things that happened after the summer of 2002. On September 2, 2002, the French doping investigation was finally, officially closed. Bill Stapleton was right—it went away quietly. After 21 months of inquiry, investigators admitted they'd found not a

shred of proof, and they issued just a small discourteous announcement from the prosecutor's office. The case was dropped for lack of
evidence.

We had a party at Milagro to celebrate the six-year anniversary
of my cancer diagnosis, and, after the fact, my 31st birthday. Children ran everywhere. The girls crawled around on the lawn while I
put Luke on a four-wheeler and drove him around. We had barbecue, cases of Shiner Bock beer, and two cakes, one that said CARPE,
and one that said DIEM.

The girls began to walk, and Kik painted their toenails pink. That
fall, Luke started preschool. By then he was a seasoned world traveler,
so his first trip to school was no problem. He bolted into class with a
wave, and he got an excellent report in his first parent-teacher conference: he was lively and played nice with the other kids. "He par-
ticipates, and he's outgoing," the teacher said. "He's the leader of the
class, and friends with everybody. And he loves the girls."

When I got home, we sat down to dinner and discussed the day.
I said to Luke, "Do you like your dinner?"

"Yeah, I like my dinner."

"I also hear you like chicks."

"Yeah. Chicks for dinner," he said.

As he grows, Luke has more and more questions, and I just try
to have good answers. But there are things I struggle to answer for
myself, let alone for him and for his sisters.

In February of 2003, Kik and I agreed to a trial separation, and
we entered marriage counseling. I moved into my one-room cabin at
Milagro, the small ranch that I had cleared and planted with a soft
green lawn. I sat on a rocking chair on the porch and cast around for

the specific cause of our marital difficulties, but they were cloudy to me. All I knew was that in trying to do everything, we'd forgotten to do the most important thing. We forgot to be married. It was like being in a current you didn't know was there. One day we looked up and realized we'd been swept downstream from our landmarks, all the points of reference.

People warn you that marriage is hard work, but you don't listen. You talk about the pretty bridesmaids' dresses, but you don't talk about what happens next; about how difficult it will be to stay, or to rebuild. What nobody tells you is that there will be more than just some hard days. There will be some hard weeks and perhaps even some hard years.

In February I returned to Europe for training alone, and Kik stayed behind in Austin. But we continued to talk and to work at rebuilding our relationship with a better foundation. In April, Kik came to Europe and we went to Nice, where we had lived together before we were married. It was the first time in four years that we had really been alone, without children.

As of this writing, we didn't know what the future would hold, but we did know this: we intended to bring the same dedication and discipline to counseling that we brought to the rest of our lives. And whatever our personal shortcomings, and no matter the outcome, the marriage is a success: we have three great prizes.

I know this, too: the seize-the-day mentality that I carried with me from the illness doesn't always serve me well. It's too tempting, in the throes of it, to quit on any problem that seems hard or inconvenient, to call it a waste of precious time and move on to something more immediate. Some things require patience.

The question of how to live through cancer, for me, has become: how do you live beyond it? Survivorship is not unlike competition; both are emotionally complicated, and neither necessarily delivers pat answers, no matter how nice it is to think so. In both cases, you have to constantly ask yourself what the real lessons are, what's worth transferring to the rest of your life?

But both cancer and competition have taught me one great, incontrovertible lesson that I think every person can learn from, whether healthy or ill, athlete or layman. The lesson is this: personal comfort is not the only thing worth seeking.

Whether the subject is bike racing, or cancer, or just living, comfort only takes us to a point that's known. Since when did sheets with the right thread-count, a coffee maker, and an electric toothbrush become the only things worth having or working toward? Too often, comfort gets in the way of inner reckonings.

For instance, there's no math that can tell you why some people ride in the Tour de France, some never enter the race, and some ride but don't risk. I've known guys who never quite put it all on the line, and you know what? They lost. One minute, after nearly a month of suffering, can decide who wins. Is it worth it? It depends on whether you want to win. I have the will to suffer. I do have that.

There are parts unknown with regard to human performance, and those are the parts when it's just about pain and forfeit. How do you make yourself do it? You remind yourself that you're fulfilling your obligation to get the best from yourself, and that all achievement is born out of sacrifice.

The experience of suffering is like the experience of exploring, of finding something unexpected and revelatory. When you find the

outermost thresholds of pain, or fear, or uncertainty, what you experience afterward is an expansive feeling, a widening of your capa-
bilities.

Pain is good because it teaches your body and your soul to improve. It's almost as though your unconscious says, "I'm going to remember this, remember how it hurt, and I'll increase my capacities so
that the next time, it doesn't hurt as much." The body literally builds
on your experiences, and a physique and temperament that have gone
through a Tour de France one year will be better the next year, because
it has the memory to build upon. Maybe the same is true of living, too.

If you lead a largely unexamined life, you will eventually hit a
wall. Some barriers can be invisible until you smack into them. The
key, then, is to investigate the wall inside yourself, so you can go beyond it. The only way to do that is to ask yourself painful questions—just as you try to stretch yourself physically.

So the fact that there are unanswered questions in my life doesn't
bother me. I don't know what happens next, and I don't need to
know, because I welcome the exploration. There's no simple and final explanation for me. Can't be, won't be. As I watch my children
grow, it occurs to me that while the structure of your bones takes
shape, other elements leave their tracings on you, too. I can see that
in my own scars—there's no way to move through this life and not
be marked by the unexpected.

As we move, we leave trails, intended or not. Trails of action,
trails of sound, trails of colors, trails of light. Who knows how long
they last?

When I climb out of the water at Dead Man's Hole, I walk over
the rocks, and if I turn and look behind me, what I see are my own

damp footprints disappearing. They disappear before my eyes. When I look in front of me, what do I see? I see the turning of more of these pages, and in the pages there will be near things, small things, fuck-ups, celebrations, tragedies, broodings, weddings, graduations, accidents, and close calls.

I want to feel this life as it occurs. Not as it *might* have occurred. Or as it *could* have been, if only. I want to feel it, *as it is*: naked or clothed; barefoot or wearing shoes; cold, hot, complicated, simple, fearful, happy, discontented, exhilarated, fruitful, selfish, giving, and feeling.

All I know is that I shouldn't be alive, and yet I feel more alive than just about anyone. Each time I go back to Dead Man's Hole, I do the jump again. I still believe a little fear is good for you. I believe it so much that after a while, when the jump became routine, I began to study a higher point on the rocks.

This is an outcropping that offers a truly terrifying 50-foot drop to the water. For days I regarded it with my friends, and we made laughing bets about whether any of us would ever have the nerve to do it. Finally, one afternoon, my friend Morris Denton did it. He threw himself off that shelf of rock and arrowed down into the cold green water, and as he came up we all shrieked and applauded. Next, Ryan Street jumped off, and plummeted into the water.

I crept to the edge, and peered over. As I stood there, I felt the blood rush from my head into my feet, and I got weak. "No way," I called down, my voice echoing. "I can't do it." I stepped carefully back, retreating from the cliff.

Down below, Morris treaded water. "What's the matter?" he called.

"I can't do it," I yelled down.

"You scared, Mellow *Janey*?"

I stopped short. Ryan and Morris's high-pitched howls of laughter caromed off the stone canyon walls. "*Mellow Janey! Mellow Janey!*"

"That's funny," I yelled.

I stood there for a moment, laughing with them. And then I turned around . . . and ran straight off the edge of the cliff.

I threw myself into the air. The rock ledge dropped out from under me, and for a fraction of a second I hung in the breeze, my arms pinwheeling and my legs kicking involuntarily, with nothing below but green water. The breath died in my throat. My friends stared upward, open-mouthed and laughing, at a man thrilled to be in midair . . .

LANCE ARMSTRONG
FOUNDATION

Afterword

I've said it many times before—if I had to choose between winning the Tour de France or having cancer, I'd choose cancer. I consider myself lucky for the experience, and because of that I feel a strong commitment to fulfill the "obligation of the cured." That's why I created the Lance Armstrong Foundation (LAF). The LAF is dedicated to helping the *nine million* cancer survivors who are dealing with all the same issues I am.

Today, seven years after my cancer diagnosis, the LAF is just as important to me as the day I signed it into existence. Cancer changed my life. From the moment I was diagnosed, priorities changed and focus shifted. I had lots of new challenges to meet— physically, psychologically, and socially. That is why the LAF is dedicated to enhancing the quality of life for those living with, through, and beyond cancer. Life after cancer is all about living, and the LAF wants to help make sure cancer survivors and their loved ones experience the highest quality of life possible.

Thanks to advances in medicine and science, we've come to a time where the odds in favor of living long past a cancer diagnosis are increasingly brighter. Unfortunately, most programs fail to recognize the particular needs of cancer survivors beyond diagnosis and treatment. I know firsthand how relevant and important these issues are, and I consider myself very fortunate to have had access to so many experts and resources to help me make informed decisions about my life after my diagnosis. The LAF works hard to create this same level of access for all cancer survivors and help fill that void in survivorship services and information.

For me, there were four things that really helped me face the ongoing challenges of cancer: knowledge, support, motivation, and hope. I want to extend these four gifts to all cancer survivors, so they too can face head-on the life changes that cancer brings. The LAF works to achieve this by providing education about the immediate and long-term challenges of managing cancer.

The LAF promotes the optimal physical, psychological, and social recovery and care of cancer survivors. We do the same for their loved ones. We focus our efforts in four areas: survivorship education and resources, community programs, national advocacy initiatives, and scientific and clinical research grants. We educate cancer survivors, healthcare professionals, and the general public about cancer survivorship issues; aid in the development of services and support for survivors; address health-policy issues to increase services for cancer survivors; and support research for a better understanding of cancer and cancer survivorship.

I'm thrilled by the success that the LAF continues to exhibit. Since I created the Foundation in 1997, it has raised more than $23 million in funding for cancer survivorship programs and grants. Our revenues have grown from less than $250,000 in 1997 to more than $7 million in 2002. In that time, we have invested our resources in many innovative cancer survivorship programs, grants, and mission-related activities and helped countless cancer survivors and their loved ones.

I invite you to join us in our important mission—enhancing the quality of life for those living with, through, and beyond cancer. With your help, we'll continue to make a difference for cancer survivors and to awaken the spirit of hope in all of us. There are a lot of ways that you can help: volunteering, joining our Peloton Project, donating, or raising awareness. For more information, please call the Lance Armstrong Foundation at (512) 236–8820, or visit www.laf.org. Thanks for your support.

. . . Another Ending . . .

You think it's over, and then it's not. I thought I was done with this book, which was supposed to be about overcoming odds, not just in one period of your life, but the whole of it. What happened next was, I set out to win a fifth Tour de France, and got knocked on my ass, and was reminded of just how hard it can be to get back up. Which is exactly the point: you don't just overcome odds once and that's it. Things keep, you know, happening.

In the 2003 Tour, things kept happening. Too many things. There were crashes, heat waves, viruses, broken bikes, such a succession of miseries that the event began to seem jinxed. At one point, I stood on a mountainside in the Pyrenees, cut, bruised, and screaming, because I was certain the race was lost. At times the only thing that kept me riding was, as race announcer Phil Liggett described it, "the magnetism of a finish line."

Is history an actual force? It felt like it. In the 100th anniversary edition of the Tour, it seemed I was riding against some eerie invisible opponent. It was as if the collective spirit and judgment of the past greats got together and decided that this year's winner had to prove not just his worthiness, but his ability to deal with the absurd and near-unendurable.

I should have known it would be a hard race when, a couple of days before it began, a bird soiled Johan's shoulder. We were sitting outside the team bus having a meeting when it splattered on his shirt. Was it a bad omen? In some countries it's considered a good one. Later, there would be a lot of discussion about good luck, and bad. But to me, that's excuse-making. The fact is, in the previous four years I'd won the race without having to overcome any real misfortunes: no crashes, no flats, no problems. Now things went wrong all at once—or maybe they just evened out.

It started in the winter, when Kik and I separated. Anyone who has been through something similar understands how catastrophic it is emotionally, and how it overwhelms any other concern. I tried to tell myself that I was managing the situation and that my personal trials had nothing to do with the bike, but it worked on me. I never cracked physically, had a day where I couldn't get out of bed or get on the bike. But it was a disruption, and I don't mean a disruption in training. It was a disruption in my head and my heart.

As the Tour approached, there were other, smaller problems. I crashed in an important tune-up race for the Tour, called the Dauphiné Libéré, on Friday the 13th ironically, and was slow to recover. I came down with tendinitis in my hip. I caught a stomach bug from my kids the week I was supposed to leave for Paris and barely made the trip. I was still doubled over the day before the race began.

As I prepared for the Prologue, I told myself maybe I could still find my form on the road once the race began. But everyone expected another big, dominating victory from me, more than they had in any other year. When you hear that all the time, it gets to you, and you begin to feel that there isn't much to race for. You can only lose.

I promptly lost. I finished seventh in the Prologue, and started the Tour in a full-blown crisis. Now everybody knew what I'd hoped to hide: word immediately swept through the peloton that I wasn't the rider I'd been in the past. My performance bolstered the hopes of every rider that night, including those of Jan Ullrich, who showed up in Paris looking as lean and fit as he ever had, and riding for a new team, Bianchi.

From there, things just got worse. The very first stage, to Meaux, was marked by an epic crash. The peloton was jumpy and tightly packed as we raced for the finish, and one small event caused a huge chain reaction. A guy came out of his pedal. That's all. Within seconds, 176 riders piled into each other, total carnage. The worst casualty of the day was my friend and neighbor Tyler Hamilton, who broke his right collarbone but somehow got up and kept riding. I was luckier; I had some bruises and road rash. But the crash signaled what kind of race it would be.

So did the heat. It was hot all across France, very hot, and it made the race hard for everybody. In the early sprinting stages, the heat rose to 100 degrees and beat down on our heads and shoulders. It was like being leaned on by something heavy and it steadily sapped me. Instead of feeling better as the days went on, if anything, I felt weaker.

But my teammates carried me through the first week. Postal won a wonderful collective stage victory, a team time trial from Joinville to St. Dizier of 42.9 miles. It was a highly technical stage that required all nine riders to go flat-out, together, against the clock. We yearned to show that Postal had become the best team in a European-dominated sport, and we rode perfectly, a flying blue wedge of speed.

We won the stage in 1 hour, 18 minutes, and 27 seconds, half a minute faster than our closest competitors, and that vaulted me from 12th place into second. Just as satisfying was the fact that Postal riders occupied the top eight places in the overall standings, and I actually trailed my own teammate, Victor Hugo Peña, who claimed the yellow jersey. As we'd neared the finish line, we were all tired, but I urged Victor on, saying, "What color do you want to wear tonight? What color?"

After a week of riding, we were heading into the Alps and I still didn't feel great. I kept telling myself that it was a long race, and I waited to feel strong again, but anyone who knew me could see that I was struggling—especially when we arrived at Alpe d'Huez for the eighth stage. In the past I'd taken control of the Tour in the Alps, and the presumption was that I'd mount another huge attack. But Alpe d'Huez was the site of yet another mishap, and a reckoning.

The stage included a monstrous climb up the Galibier, a 30-kilometer ascent that was among the highest in the Alps. I felt uncharacteristically leg-weary as we climbed, and I couldn't understand it. Finally, on the descent, I looked down and realized that my back brake was rubbing against my wheel.

On the radio, I called Johan. "Johan, I have good news and bad news," I said.

His voice crackled. "Okay, tell me the good news first."

"No, I'm going to tell you the bad news first. The bad news is, I feel like shit. The good news is, I think I know why. I just looked back and my brake has been rubbing the whole time."

I'd ridden the first 120 kilometers or so of the stage with the brake on. It was like trying to swim in a pair of boots. It was almost embarrassing; I should've noticed sooner.

I fixed the bike problem, but I couldn't fix the body problem. I was tired. It was 100 degrees again, and now we were heading into the final climb up Alpe d'Huez, and other riders started attacking. There went Joseba Beloki. There went a talented young Spaniard named Iban Mayo. There went the rising Russian star Alexandre Vinokourov. There went my friend Tyler Hamilton, riding with his broken collarbone.

I couldn't chase them. I struggled up the mountain and finished fourth. It put me in the overall lead, but it was hardly the dominant performance that people had expected. The numbers didn't lie: my personal time up Alpe d'Huez was four minutes slower than it had been in 2001. I had the yellow jersey, but it was bittersweet; I knew I wasn't the strongest rider that day, and I had to face the fact that I wasn't riding well and could lose the race.

The next day we journeyed from Bourg d'Oisans to Gap, and again the attacks kept coming. Vinokourov, Mayo, and Beloki pounded at me. The heat was so intense by now that the tar roads were melting, which made the dueling that much more intense—and dangerous, too.

What happened next was one of those instances when good luck and bad collided in the same moment. Finally, we reached the last big descent of the stage. We whirled into a corner that was sticky and slick with tar. Beloki was intent on chasing down a break by Vinokourov, and I hung back, 15 yards behind him. We came into the turn at about 50 miles an hour.

Beloki's wheel started to slide.

He tried to brake—and his wheel locked. Then it caught hard, and the bike jerked, and went over to the side.

Beloki was whipsawed off the bike. He slammed onto the pavement right in front of me. Man and machine skidded across the road, tangled up together.

I tried to brake—and now my rear wheel started to lock up, too. I was losing it. I had two choices: I could either pile into Beloki, or swerve off the road. I swerved.

I hurtled into a field. I had no idea what had happened to Beloki behind me. All I knew was that I was lucky to still be upright. There could have been a cliff at the side of that road, or a wall. Instead, there was an open field. I was lucky, too, that the field had been harvested and wasn't full of crops.

The bike jounced over tractor furrows and broken stalks. I thought about trying to turn around, but that would cost me precious time. I glanced up and saw that the road hairpinned back toward me. I thought, *Maybe I can off-road through the field and pick up the race route again.* On instinct, I veered sharply and kept going, wheeling over crunchy stalks, certain that at any moment I would go over the handlebars, or get a flat tire. Finally, I got across the field. There was the road.

Suddenly, there was a ditch, a rain gutter. I braked hard, almost plunging into it headfirst. There was no way around it, so I jumped off the bike and hoisted it over my shoulder, potato-sack style. I leaped across the rain gutter. My back foot slid about two feet, and kicked up a cloud of dust as I jumped.

I landed on the other side, ran to the road, and vaulted back on my bike. Just then, Tyler sped by me and waved, a kind of salute. I pedaled to catch up with the lead group. I rode on, relieved to still be in the race.

I finished the stage in decent shape, still in the yellow jersey. But I felt lousy for Beloki. That evening, I called his team doctor, a gentleman named Pedro Celaya, to see how he was doing, and found out he'd broken his thigh, wrist, and elbow. Celaya was in the hospital visiting with Beloki when I called, and I passed along my sincere regrets, "I'm really sorry this happened," I said. "Tell him I thought he looked great." I meant it. You never want to see a great competitor put out of the race by a crash. Accidents like that don't help the contest.

Afterward, Beloki and I became comrades of sorts. For the rest of the Tour, he would call Johan every now and again to say good luck and pass on his best wishes.

I hoped the trip into the field was my last mishap—surely nothing more could go wrong. But it was just the opposite. A couple of days later, I took the start line in a critical stage, an individual time trial of 47 kilometers from Gaillac to Cap'Découverte. Again, the sun was intense, and as I warmed up, I sweated through my clothes. I already felt sapped and thirsty as I waited in the starting gate. Ahead, I knew Jan Ullrich was riding a fast time.

I shot out of the gate and hunched down over my racing bars. At first, everything went okay, but it was so hot that I kept pulling at my water bottle. A third of the way around the course, Ullrich and I were dead even.

But now the heat was inside my helmet, and inside my racing skins, and I couldn't seem to cool off. I drank and drank. Dehydration starts days before it really hits you. Now it hit me: suddenly I was parched, and powerless.

Then I ran out of water.

At the second time check, I'd lost 39 seconds to Ullrich, and I was slowing. There was no way to get more water; time-trial rules forbid a rider to get help on the course. I didn't care what my split times were anymore. I just wanted to drink.

By the time I hit the finish line, I'd lost a minute and 36 seconds to Ullrich, and there was a huge ring of white salt around my mouth. I slumped off the bike. I'd lost nearly 15 pounds in fluids in a single ride. Somehow I'd hung on for second place, and I still wore yellow, but I was a very shaky, ill leader.

I didn't know how to face my teammates. Johan just patted me and said, "Look, we'll get it back tomorrow." But dinner that night was quiet. I could almost hear the guys wondering what was going to happen, whether I still had it in me to win the race. I felt miserable, and guilty. The boys in blue were working tirelessly on my behalf, and I wasn't able to make their hard work pay off. Instead, every day seemed to bring some new mishap, and now I'd failed physically on a crucial stage. I could barely look at them. But no one whispered or complained, or questioned aloud. They just ate their meals and kept their jaws tightly shut and went about their work.

The next morning, as we rode into the Pyrenees, George rolled up next to me. I was still at rock bottom, and George could see it. "I just want you to know something," he said.

"What? I suck?"

"No. What you did yesterday may be the most impressive thing I've seen you do."

"Why?"

"Because I could see that you were suffering, and you hung in there."

George's words helped me through the wretched day ahead. We were now entering the most difficult mountain stages of the entire Tour, and I was in no shape to defend a lead. When you have severe dehydration, you can't recover from it in a day, or even two. That day we had a hard climb to a village called Bonascre, and I was going to suffer badly. I knew it—and so did everyone else.

By the end of that day I'd lost more time to Ullrich. Now he was just 15 seconds behind me.

At the finish, I looked terrible again. I had sunken eyes, and I looked old. Word around the peloton was that I couldn't hang on much longer; that I was going to lose the Tour any day now to Ullrich.

Through it all, my teammates kept me going, with the help of Johan. None of them panicked. Instead, Johan insisted that I would eventually feel stronger, and that Ullrich was bound to weaken at some point. He also looked for some practical ways to protect our lead. He came up with an inspired tactic to help defend me from constant attacks other riders were launching: he decided to turn the tables. He sent our climbers, Chechu and Manuel Beltrán (whom we called "Tricki," which is Spanish for Cookie Monster), on the attack. They shot up the road, forcing other riders to chase them. It worked: the other riders were so busy chasing Tricki and Chechu, they couldn't attack me. I was able to ride at a more comfortable pace.

Then one day, as Johan had promised, I did begin to feel a little better. Johan swore he could see my pedaling getting stronger. "You've worked hard and you're prepared," he said. "Things have gone wrong, but in the last week of the Tour it's the experience, the mentality, and the determination that make a difference, and I don't think anybody is stronger in those three things than you." He still believed in me—and that helped me believe.

Breakfasts and dinners continued to be quiet, grim affairs, with everyone determined to preserve our slim lead. I just needed one big day, I told myself.

But I needed it soon—practically overnight, in fact. We now had just one final climbing stage, to a summit called Luz Ardiden. If I was going to win the Tour, I'd have to do it there.

Fear gnawed at me: what if I lost, after all we'd been through in the race? When you carry the hopes and expectations of a team, you feel a lot of responsibility. I was carrying other things, too. In the middle of the Pyrenean stages, shortly before Luz Ardiden, Kik sent me a text message. She'd had a dream that I was riding up a mountain. But hitched to the back of my bike was a cart, and in the cart were people—cancer survivors, sponsors, well-wishers—and I was trying to pull all of them up the hill. In her dream, she wrote, I unhooked the harness and rode away. "Throw off the weights that are holding you back," she urged.

Kik was right. I was trying to pull this thing along, and feeling too much weight. It was a message that meant a lot, and I saved it.

On the evening before Luz Ardiden, Bill Stapleton came to visit me, and he told me something else that encouraged me. We talked about how close the race was, and how much pressure I was feeling. Bill just stared at me calmly, and said, "Dude, you're the guy who makes the eight ball."

I didn't know what he meant. "The eight ball," I repeated.

"Clear the table," he said. "Eight ball, corner pocket. You call it, you make it."

That night, I slept soundly, and the next morning, I woke up feeling well, better than I had since the Tour began. I went down to the team bus for a cup of coffee. "I think I'm back," I told Johan.

I sipped my coffee and thought about Luz Ardiden. Ullrich and his

Bianchi team director, Rudy Pevenage, were telling everyone that he would lead the race by the time we reached the summit. I was going to lose the Tour that day, thanks to them, they said.

As I sat on the bus still sipping coffee and thinking, one of our operations managers, Geert Duffy, came over and told me a story. The year before, Pevenage had asked him for a souvenir yellow jersey. Duffy had promised to get one for him, but then forgot. Now that Ullrich was within 15 seconds of me, Pevenage had gone looking for Duffy.

"Hey, Duffy—don't worry about that jersey," he said, "because we're going to get our own."

I listened as Duffy told me the story. I put my cup down.

"The Tour is over," I said. And I walked out of the bus.

It helped to know their plans. Now I had plans of my own. At the start line, I saw Tyler Hamilton. "Be ready," I said. " 'Cause I'm going."

It was my last chance. After Luz Ardiden, there would be just one more critical stage, a time trial to Nantes, and Ullrich had already beaten me once in a time trial. I didn't want to go to Nantes with only a 15-second lead. I needed to gain some time in this final mountaintop stage.

It was perhaps the longest, hardest climbing day of the Tour. When we passed over the massive Tourmalet, Ullrich briefly got away, with a shock attack. I decided not to waste energy going after him, but preferred to let him work. Gradually, I reeled him in again as his tempo slowed. We fell back into a group with Mayo and Vinokourov and swung down into another descent.

Finally, after five hours on the bikes, we reached the foot of Luz Ardiden—and the pace quickened, and a kind of sparring match on bikes began.

Iban Mayo attacked. I leaped up and countered the attack, and passed him.

Now I was in front. I darted up the road. Where was Ullrich? I wondered. I hoped he was paying for the Tourmalet.

In my ear Johan said calmly, "Ullrich is dropped."

Behind me, Ullrich lagged, pain on his face. He churned upward, but he couldn't match the acceleration. "Ten seconds," Johan said. I felt a small bloom of excitement.

I lunged at the pedals, scaling the mountain, thinking about putting empty road between myself and Ullrich. I hugged the side of the route, cutting every corner. I skimmed past spectators, barely noticing them . . .

A flash of yellow caught my eye. A small kid was holding a yellow Tour souvenir bag, whipping it back and forth.

Uh-oh, I'm going to catch that thing, I thought.

Suddenly, the bag was tangled on the handle of my brake. I felt the bike jerk violently beneath me—

It flipped over sideways.

It was as though I had been garroted. I went straight down, and landed on my right hip, hard. *I've crashed? Now?* I thought, incredulously. *How could I have crashed?*

My next thought was, *Well, the Tour's over. It's too much, too many things gone wrong.*

But another thought intruded.

Get up.

It was the same thought that had prodded me during all those long months I'd spent in a hospital bed. After surgery. *Get up.* After chemo. *Get up.* It had whispered to me, and nudged me, and poked me, and now here it was again. *Get . . . up.*

I got up. Johan said later it looked as though I'd bounced back to my feet almost instantaneously, like a pop-up toy. I hauled my bike upright and worked furiously at the chain, which had come off—shaking it, threading it back onto the ring. As I did so, I began to scream, a guttural, primal roar. I screamed in fury, and in devastation. I screamed every cuss word I knew. I screamed because I thought I had lost the race.

I got the chain on, and I hopped on the bike and started to push off, and now there was a Postal mechanic behind me, shoving me up the road, and I could hear him screaming, too, with effort, and with anger.

Chechu had waited for me. Now he sped up and motioned frantically for me to follow him. I leaped up and hammered at the pedals. But the gear slipped, and my foot popped out of the pedal. The bike swung crazily, and I landed, chest first, on the top-tube of the bike. Later, I would discover that the rear chainstay was broken. Somehow I stayed upright and clipped my foot back in.

Ahead, Tyler Hamilton was angry, too. Tour etiquette dictated that the leaders wait for me to catch up, just as I had waited for Ullrich when he went off the road in that frightening crash two years previous. The Tour was supposed to be won by the strongest rider, not the luckiest, and the consensus in the peloton was that no one should profit from a freak accident.

Afterward, Ullrich would be credited with sportsmanship for waiting. But in retrospect I'm not so sure he did wait. In replays, he seems to me to be riding race tempo. He didn't attack, but he didn't wait, either—not until Tyler accelerated in front and waved at them to slow down, and yelled, "Hold up!"

The lead group slowed. Meanwhile, Johan pulled up alongside me, to see if I was all right. I had a gash on my elbow. Johan rolled down his window and started to say something. I swung my head toward him and threw him a look of pure fire. Johan closed his mouth, and closed the window without saying a word. He had seen all he needed to. "I knew then it was over," he said later.

The bike ran up the road beneath me. After just a few minutes of furious effort, I rejoined the lead group.

No sooner had I gotten there than Mayo glanced back at me—and attacked again. I immediately jumped out of the saddle, charged up to his wheel, and slingshotted past him.

I was livid. I drove my legs into the pedals, adrenaline and fear and frustration in every stroke.

In a matter of moments, I was alone. I had bolted away from the group so suddenly that nobody could follow. Once again, Ullrich receded behind me.

"He's dropped," Johan reported. "You have ten seconds."

I accelerated, almost snarling. I rode fueled by residual fright and rage from the crash. And by pent-up resentment from weeks of crashes and ordeals, and doubts.

"Twenty seconds," Johan said, more excitedly.

I found a rhythm and began to dance on the pedals, as if I were running up a staircase. "Thirty seconds . . ."

I was thirsty again. I had dropped my bottle in the crash, and now I was beginning to tire. But Johan pulled up behind me and started yelling, so excited that I could barely understand him.

"Come on, come on! This is it! You're winning the Tour! Here's your chance!"

I had given everything, and now I was wasted. The last few kilometers were one long grimace of pain. But finally the finish line was approaching, and adrenaline and anger carried me. I thought about the doubts in the peloton, all the whispers that I was too old, or too rich, or too distracted, or too American to win the Tour de France a fifth time. I thought, *This is my neighborhood, and nobody else is winning this race.*

As I crossed the line, I just slumped over my bike, my shoulders sagging, too exhausted and relieved even to lift my arms. I was bleeding and limping and drained, but I had won the stage by 40 seconds over Ullrich.

I now led the Tour by 1:07. A one-minute lead, after two weeks of suffering and self-doubt, felt like an hour. It was more than we could have expected under the circumstances. I took the podium and slipped on the yellow jersey, and as I stood there, arms upraised, I could see George crossing the finish line. My fatigue lifted, and I lit up and pointed straight at him, jabbing at the air in triumph.

Finally, I left the podium. I went to drug testing, and then the press conference, so it was some time before I finally saw Johan. I threw myself at him, and he grabbed me in a huge bear hug and shook me up and down, babbling, "Yes, yes, yes, yes!"

"This is my neighborhood," I said.

We climbed into a car together and started the drive down the mountain to our hotel. The rest of the Postals had gone ahead of us on the team bus. Suddenly I wanted to see my teammates, urgently. The only reason I had stood on the podium in the yellow jersey was because they had surrounded and protected me, and now I didn't want to ride solo, I wanted to ride with them. "Let's catch them," I said to Johan.

He sped down the road until we could see the bus ahead. We radioed the driver, and he pulled over to wait. When we reached the side of the road, I leaped out of Johan's car, ran to the bus, and clambered up the stairs. I jumped aboard and stood in the aisle, screaming in exultation.

"How do you like me now?! *How do you fucking like me now??!!*"

The guys erupted. They charged out of their seats, whooping, and for the next ten minutes it was pandemonium in the aisle, all of us hugging, crying, and pounding one another on the back.

The Tour wasn't over, but now I believed absolutely that I would win it. For the first time, I didn't feel weak or hunted. I felt like the real leader of the Tour de France. Most important, I felt I could look my teammates in the eye.

For the next three days, Ullrich and I rode in a sort of limbo, eyeing each other. There was no ground in those stages over which to make up any significant time, so we simply maintained a steady tempo and rode toward Nantes, and what we both knew would be the deciding stage, the time trial. We had nothing to do but pedal and think, and the tension grew. Every second would literally count.

We awoke in Nantes to a driving rainstorm. Nevertheless, Johan and I got up at 6:30 A.M. and drove out to examine the course. I slowly cruised up and down the road on my bike in the rain, studying the corners, train tracks, even the manholes. Just a paint mark could be dangerously slick on a wet road. The last ten kilometers were especially treacherous, I noticed—a series of roundabouts and corners that offered potential disaster. When we got back to the hotel, we heard that Ullrich had slept in, and had looked at a video of the course rather than get wet.

The team bus was quiet that morning, as the rain pelted the windows. My friend Robin Williams broke the quiet here and there with his usual hilarity, and I tried to laugh through my clenched jaw.

Eventually, all the other riders were out on the course. Reports from my teammates came back: riders were crashing every few minutes. Three of Ullrich's teammates had already gone down. I should take no chances.

Johan gave me some last tactical instructions, which amounted to a caution: I wasn't the one who needed to take risks. Ullrich was chasing me, not the other way around.

With that thought, I headed out onto the course—and started slowly. I lost six seconds to Ullrich in the first kilometer and a half.

I could feel my wheels slipping in the rain.

I stayed calm. I suspected that Ullrich had started fast to try to press me early, and maybe even demoralize me. I concentrated on my own tempo, and found a rhythm.

By the next time check, I was only two seconds back.

Ullrich kept pushing despite the fact that there was standing water all over the course. Water sprayed from our wheels on every corner.

Most of my teammates had ridden safely in, and now they were back on the bus, nervously watching the race on TV. They covered their faces with their hands as I sped over the slippery pavement. They peeked through their fingers.

I went up by ten seconds.

Ahead, Ullrich jackhammered at the pedals. He entered the most treacherous part of the course, the last ten kilometers. He swept into a roundabout.

A moment later, Johan's deadpan voice came into my ear. "Lance, Ullrich has crashed."

Ullrich had hurtled into the roundabout, and as he leaned into the curve, his bike skidded out from under him. It was as though the road had simply disappeared beneath him. He slid for a few long, terrible moments across the water-soaked asphalt, then slammed into some hay bales.

Ullrich struggled to his feet and got back on his bike, but the race was over. I was the winner of the Tour, if I could stay upright. "Lance, take it easy. Please, no risks," Johan said. "You can practically walk to the finish now and you'll still win the Tour."

From then on, my ride was a beautiful tour of Nantes. I practically sat up and enjoyed the view. But I still took care around those corners.

With three kilometers to go, Johan pulled the car up next to me and flashed a thumbs-up sign. I lifted a hand back in salute—the "hook 'em, 'horns" sign for Texas.

As I neared the finish line, all of the strain of the past three weeks fell away. I felt something almost sunny on my face and realized it was my own smile. I streaked across the line, and beat a fist in the air, and tried to absorb the moment: I was about to become a five-time winner of the Tour de France.

But records are hard to feel. They're measures, or markers, that we use to set limits. To say that someone has won five Tours is a cool abstraction, because the number doesn't begin to suggest all of the events and emotions that those races really entailed, the setbacks and the stages victories, or the anguish and the elation. Perhaps the only people who could fully understand what the phrase "five Tour de France victories" meant were my teammates, and the other four men who had done it, and they all had their own personal associations with the number five. I only knew what it meant to me: it represented the number of times I had gotten back up.

As I came down from the podium, I met Bernard Hinault. He just gripped my hand and said simply, "Welcome to the club."

The next day, the ride to Paris was a traveling ceremony. I glided along, sipped champagne, and thought about the meaning of the race: about getting up again, finding another way out of your problems, with your head or with your will. I felt a swell in my chest as we entered Paris. As we passed the Hôtel de Crillon, I saw that it was flying the Texas flag for me, as it had done for the past five years.

But the real moment of victory came that night in a private banquet room with just the team. I rose and toasted them. "This year was so hard for me, personally and professionally," I said. "I wasn't the best at times, and I know it. I scared all of us, and I promise never to let it happen again. But you guys carried me. It killed me to come down to the dinner table and look you guys in the face, after letting you down like that. After Luz Ardiden, I could finally look in your eyes with pride. I really needed you, and you were there, and now I'm here because of you. Thank you for sticking by me. I owe this jersey to you. This celebration, this night is in your honor. Thank you."

That marked the end of the 100th Tour de France for me. But like I say, things keep happening.

Kik and the kids and I returned to Girona together. We put the kids in bed, plugged in the baby monitor, and went to the café downstairs, just under our window. We ordered cold beers, Spanish ham, and bread, and we sat there in silence. We would continue to put effort, care, and deep thought into our relationship.

Over the next few days, I skipped every invitation, every interview, and every adventure. This time, unlike any other Tour victory, I just stayed home. I played with my children, and took them to the beach. We bought a new barbecue grill, and cooked outside in the garden and listened to Bob Marley. I perfected my frozen-margarita-making skills. I thought about seeing the Amalfi coast in Italy, for pleasure. For once, I didn't think about racing.

Another finish line is out there, somewhere. But I don't really want to find it—yet.